Amazing
Gel Prints

Working with Stencils

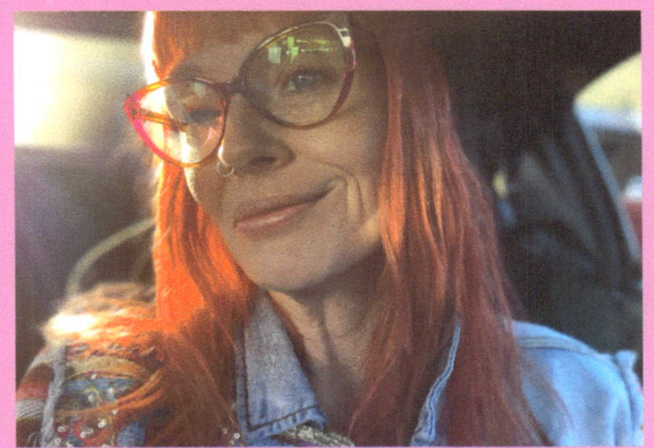

Elizabeth St. Hilaire

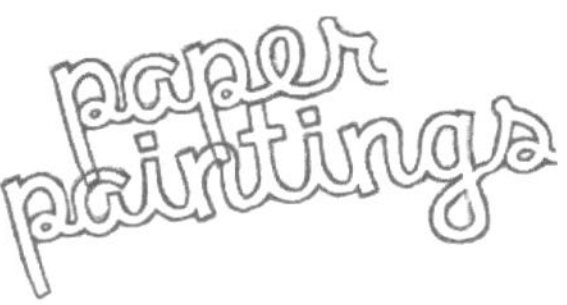

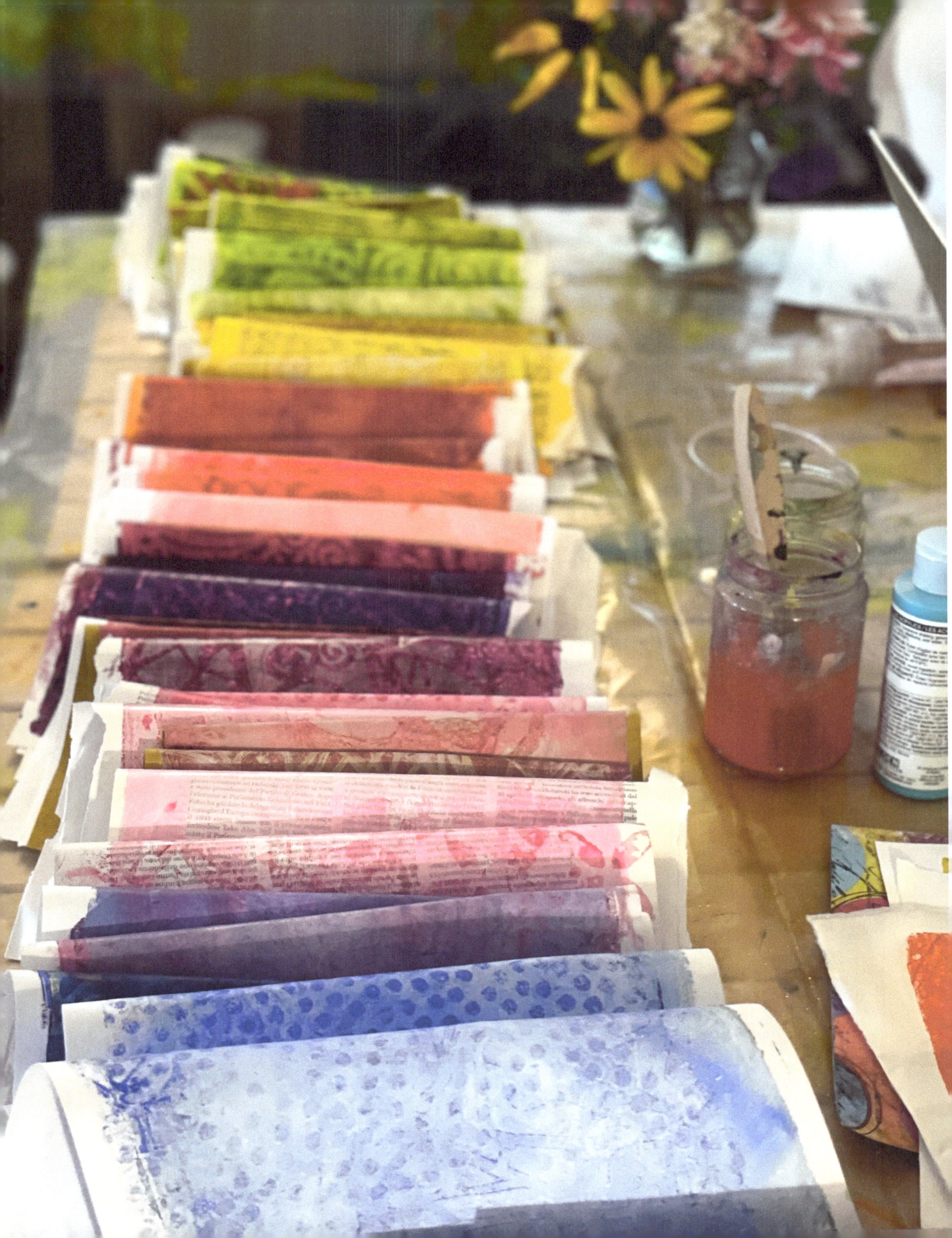

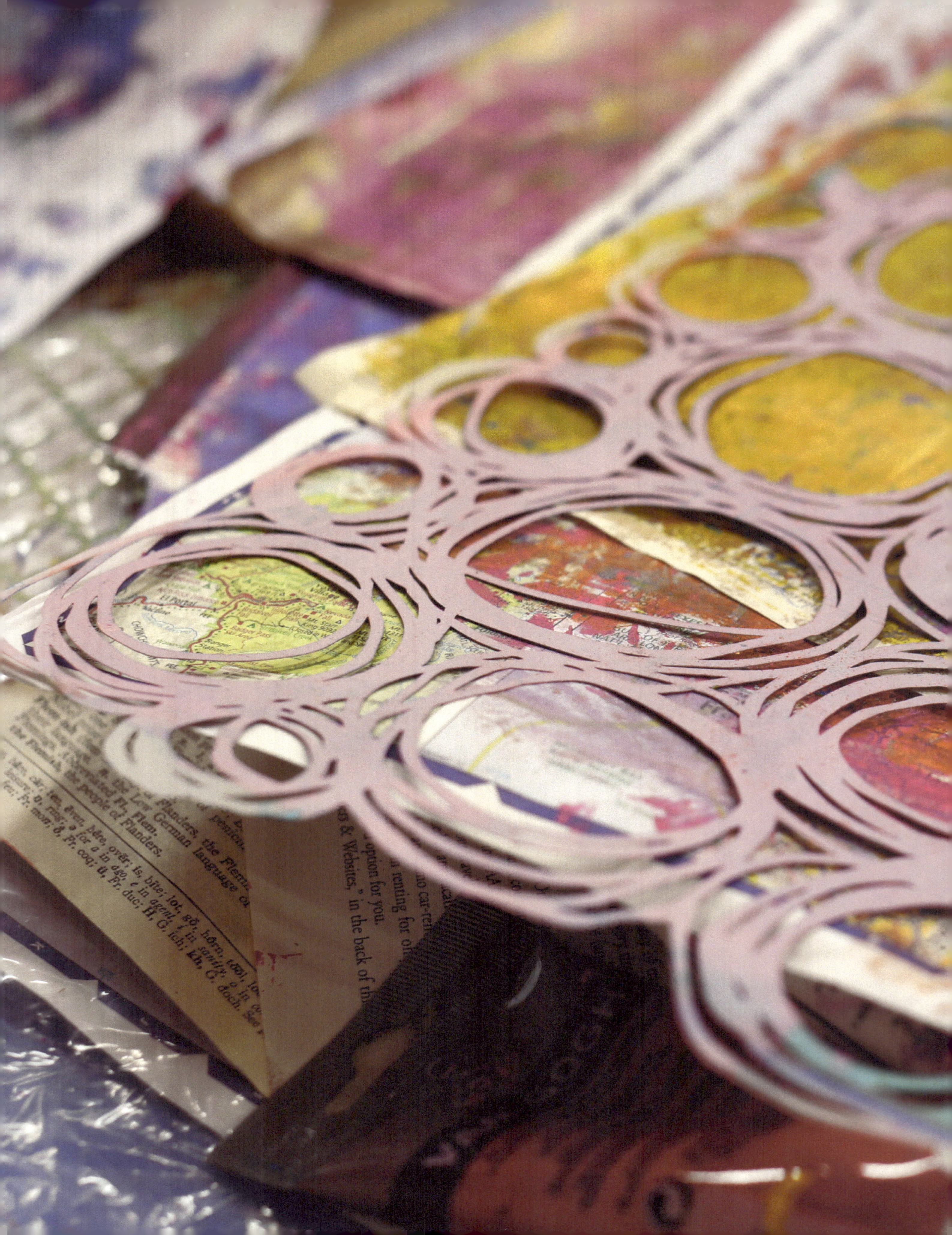

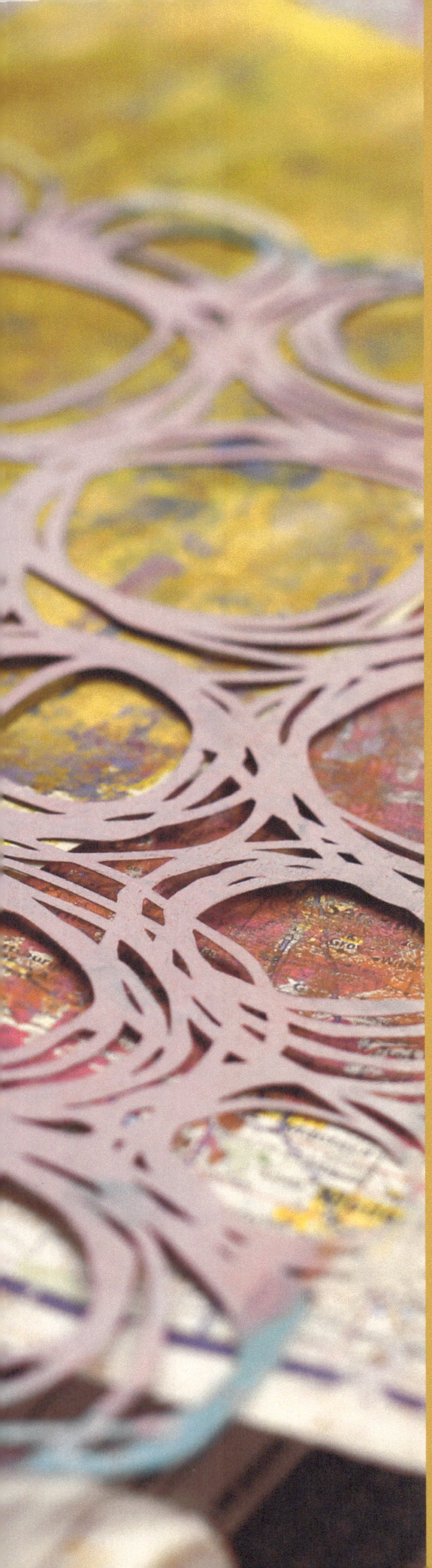

Introduction

This book offers everything you need to begin or further your skills in gel printing with stencils. The pages that follow feature techniques and tips for creating layered gel prints suitable for use in collage and mixed media projects, or as stand alone masterpieces! This book will help you develop your skills and confidence in gel printing, whether you are a beginner experimenting with the plate for the first time, or an advanced artist looking for inspiration.

The gel plate looks and feels like gelatin, but is durable, reusable, and stores at room temperature. It doesn't take up room in your fridge and it's easy to clean and always ready for printing. Monoprinting on a gel plate is simple and fun. The gratification is immediate, and the prints have endless creative applications.

Elizabeth St. Hilaire

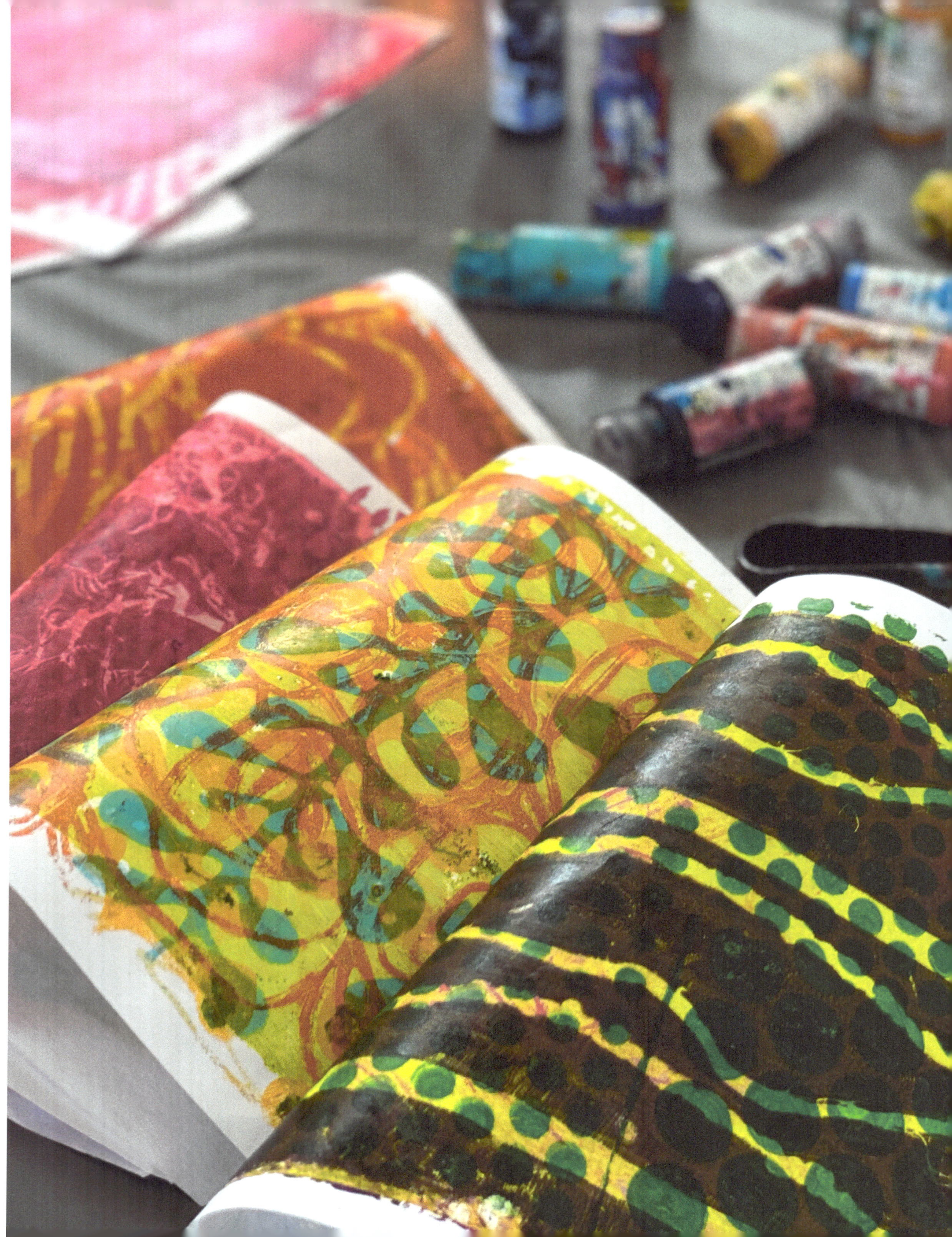

TABLE OF
Contents

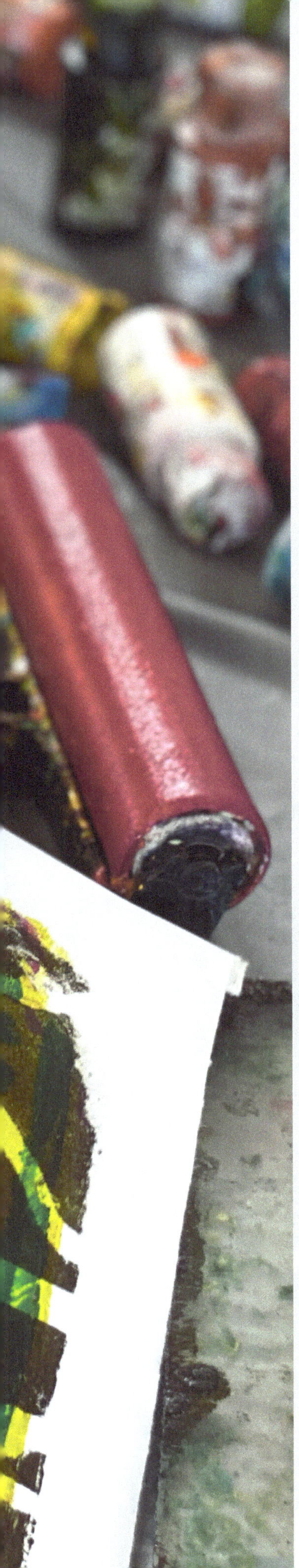

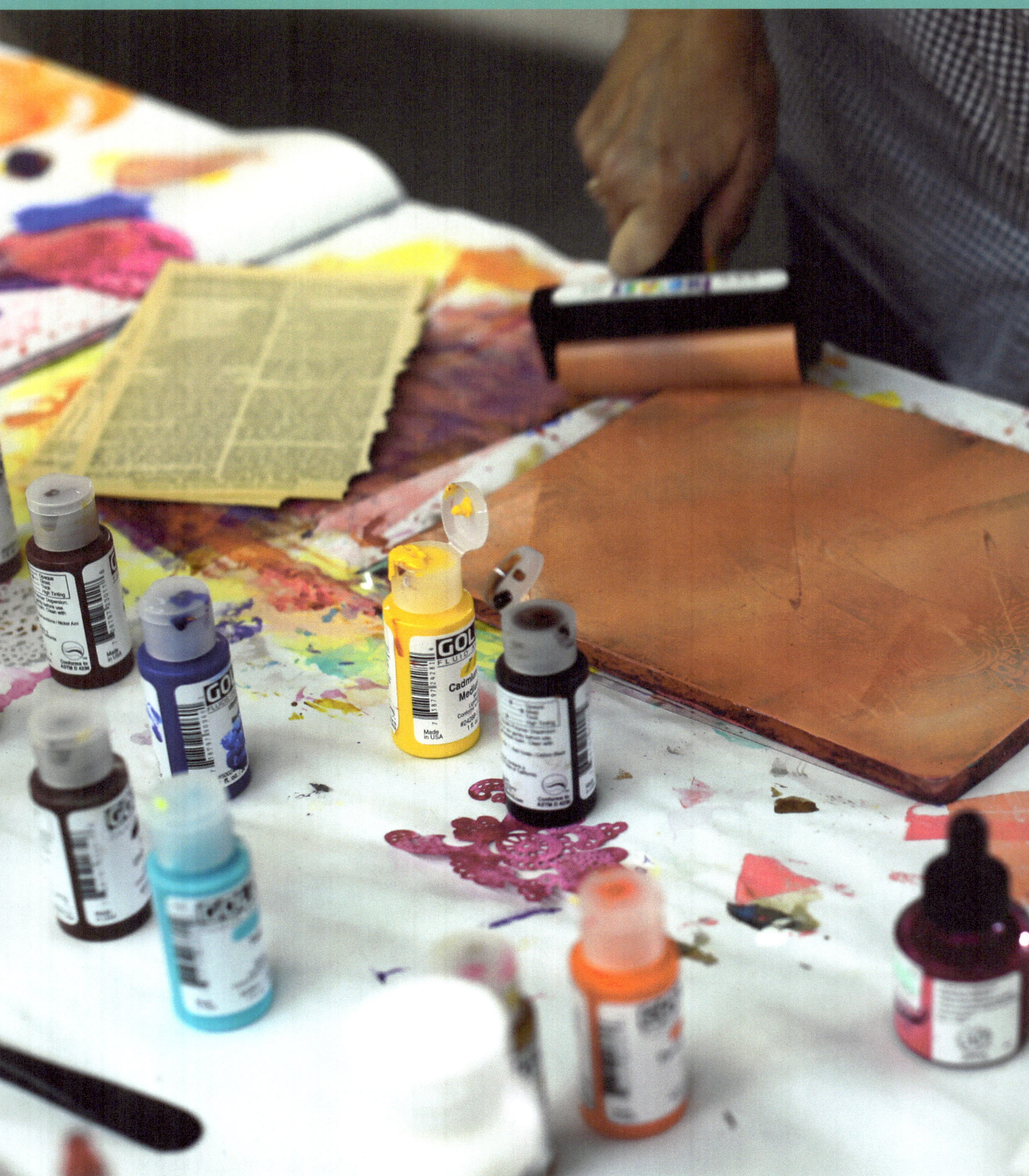

CHAPTER

1

Getting Started

Gel printing with stencils and masks is all about experimenting and giving yourself permission to play. In this section, learn about tools and materials, the basics of color theory, and creating light colored solid backgrounds as your base for subsequent layers.

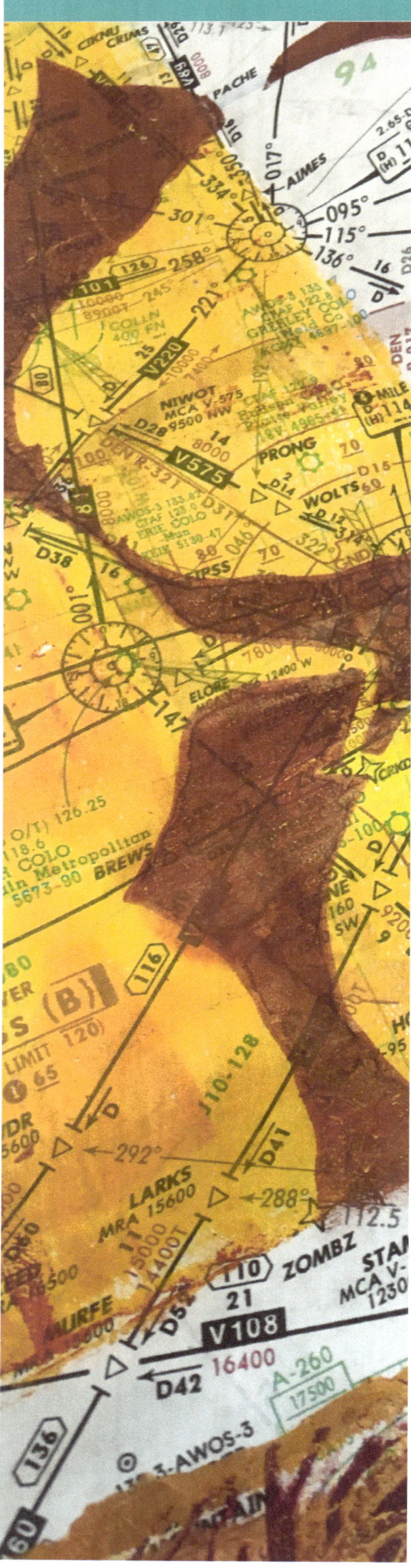

All Kinds of Paper

There are many papers that are great for Gel printing–anything from standard copy bond to card stock, from printmaking paper to rice paper, from vintage maps to old book pages, from your kids homework to decorative papers. I recommend starting out with inexpensive paper, as you get used to gel printing. You're going to go through a lot of paper!

Rice paper, on a pad or roll, is my all-time favorite for its' absorbent qualities and the way it pulls the paint from the plate. Deli paper (dry waxed paper, available on Amazon.com) works much like tissue paper due to its' translucent properties, but it is significantly more durable.

I am also a fan of found papers, so check out your local used book store or library for some old books that you can take the pages out of. This paper is often great quality, the text adds another layer to the creativity of the print making process, and the books are inexpensive.

I have learned that glossy coated paper stock is not compatible with the gel printing plate. This type of paper tends to stick to the plate and not come off without damaging the plate's surface. DO NOT use any glossy papers (including glossy photo papers).

Paper is an individual preference, and your end purpose will be a factor in your paper choice. A smooth-surfaced paper gives a more detailed print and removes the paint more completely from the surface of the printing plate.

Some of My Favorite Papers

I have found these are my all-time favorites but you should experiment with what you have on hand as well.

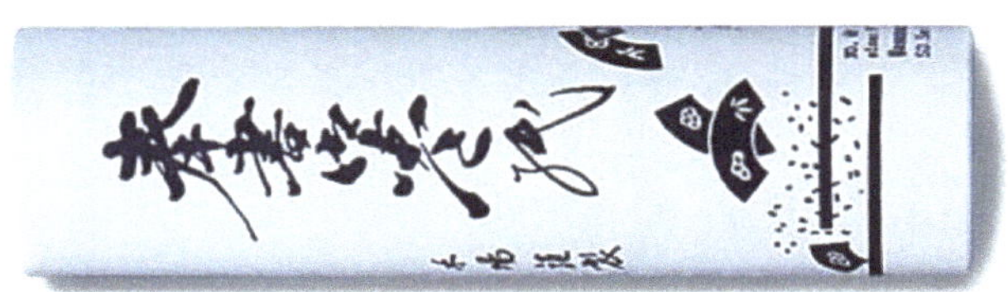

Same paper as the pad but on a roll 8"x20' sized, sturdy, absorbent rice paper

9x12, 48 sturdy sheets, sized surface, strong, absorbent rice paper–my favorite paper for printing

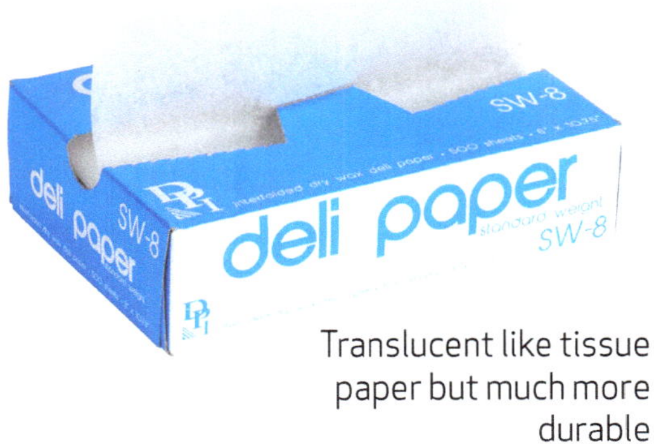

Translucent like tissue paper but much more durable

Suji Gami rice paper on a roll 18"x30' tears organically and is semi translucent, nice for layering in collage

Premium quality printer paper takes paint much better than basic copy bond

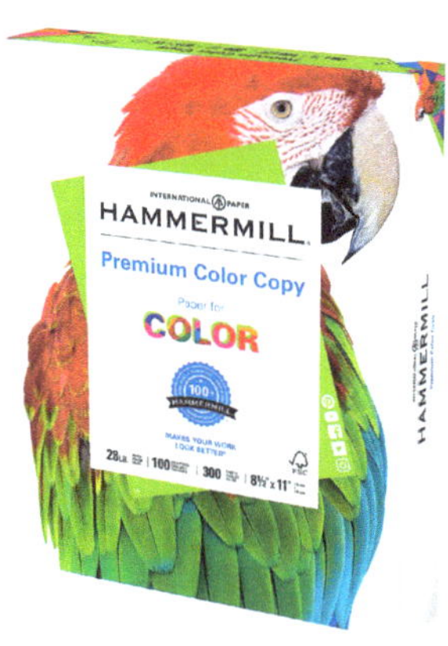

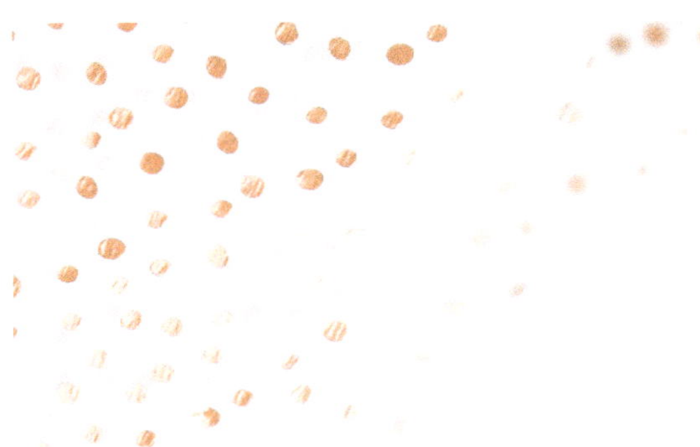

Decorative art store papers with metallic, fibers, flecks, embossing, iridescent, etc

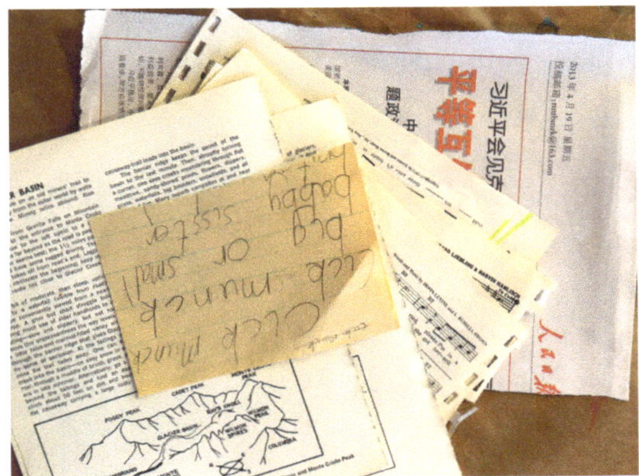

Found papers, homework, maps, books, etc.

Supplies

I have assembled a Gel Printing Amazon.com shopping list that has links to all of these products if you are looking for one-stop shopping: **Amazon.com/shop/paper-paintings-collage-artwork**

Stencils and Masks (Joggles.com)

Foam Stamps (Joggles.com)

Golden Fluid Acrylics Translucent Colors

Golden Fluid Acrylics Opaque Colors

Golden Fluid Acrylic Metallics

Golden Fluid Acrylics Interference

Rice Paper

Decorative Paper

Dry Waxed Deli Paper

Found Paper: Books, Maps, etc.

Gel Plate 9x12

Speedball Deluxe Soft Rubber Brayer 6-inch

Speedball Deluxe Soft Rubber Brayer 2-inch

Scotch Heavy Duty Clear Shipping Tape

Scrubby Soap Bar

Murphy's Oil Soap

Mini Ink Blender Tool and refills

Dish Water Basin

Jack Richeson Texture Rubbing Plates

Princeton Catalyst Wedges

Posca Paint Pens or other brand Opaque Markers

Household objects–get creative!

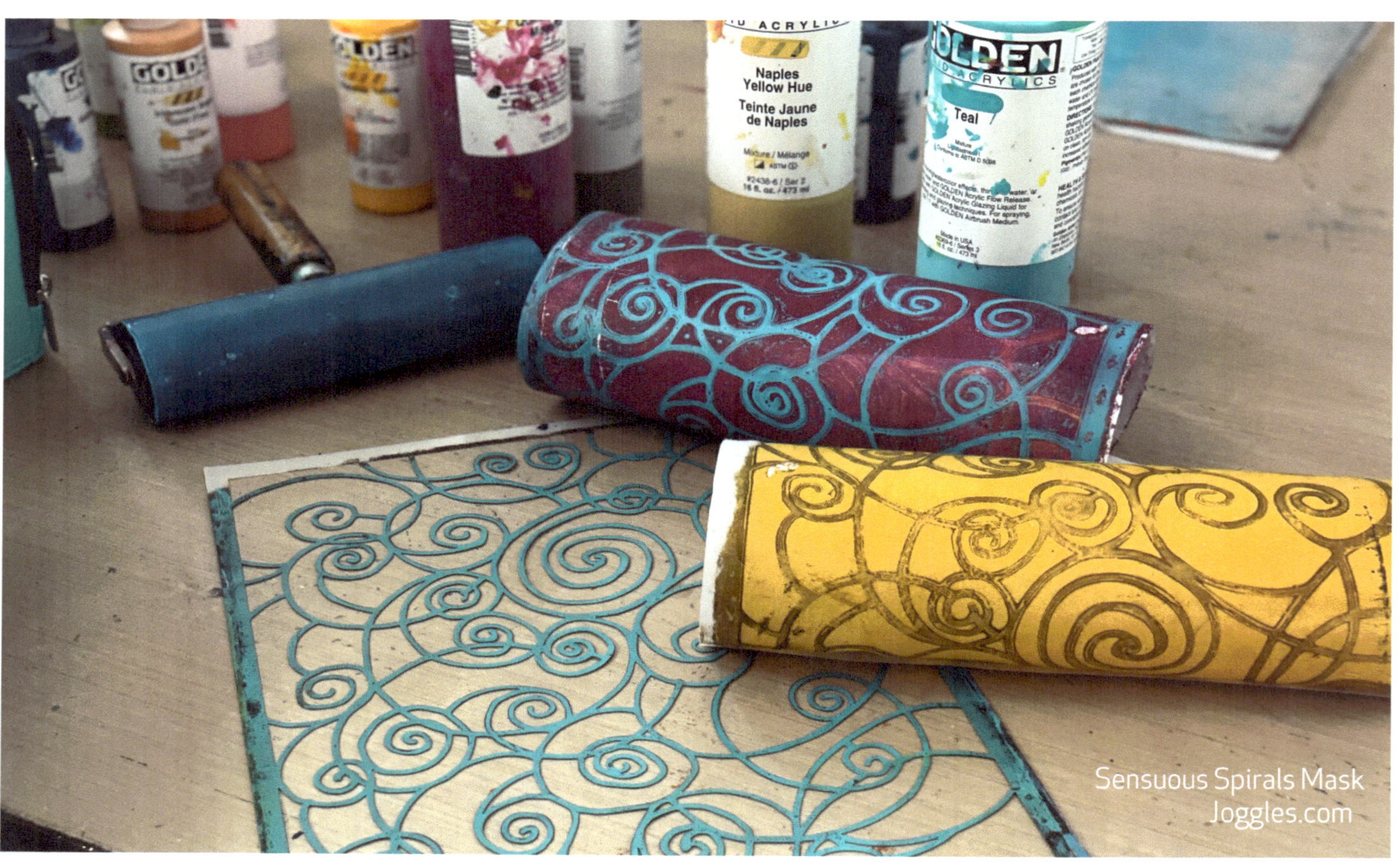

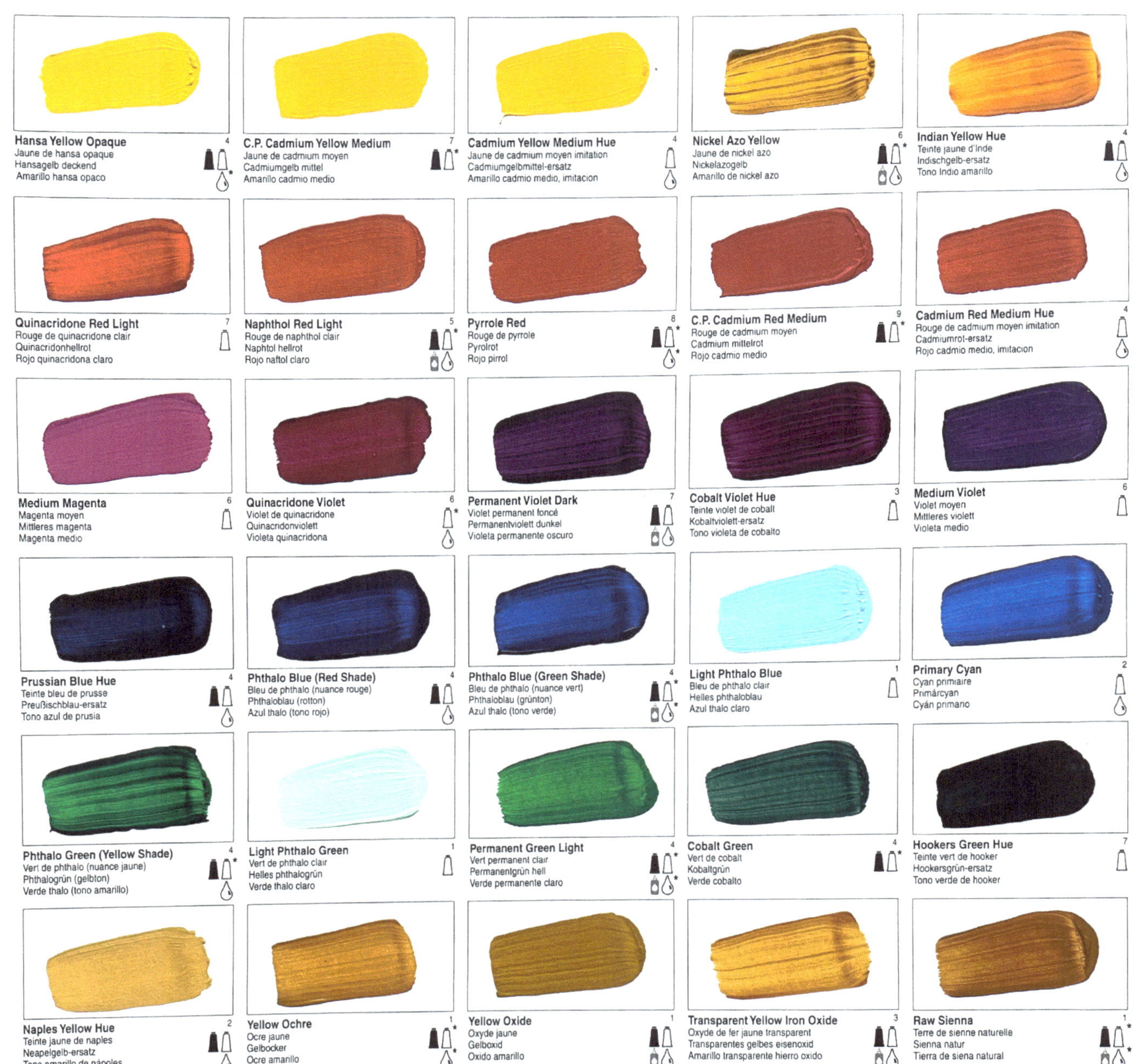

Paint

In my work I use Golden Fluid Acrylic colors exclusively to paint my papers. These paints are lightfast, durable, and flexible. They are wonderfully versatile, professional quality acrylic colors with the consistency of heavy cream. Call their customer service and request a hand painted color swatch chart for accurate color and translucency representation. Tell them I sent you! I am a trained Golden Artist Educator for Golden Paints.

Most of Golden's pigments are translucent with some exceptions, this is important to know. In this book, every layer of the monoprinting process allows the previous layer to shine through. This is the effect of translucent paints, they multiply and blend in the print. Artist-grade paints contain much more pigment and produce truer colors than inexpensive craft paints which contain more filler and are more opaque as a result.

The flip caps of Fluid Acrylics make it easier to squeeze out the appropriate amount of paint onto your plate. The viscosity of Fluid Acrylics also allows them to dry much faster than heavy body, making it easier to work more quickly with less time spent waiting.

Color

A working knowledge of color can help you create great combinations. Knowing how colors work, and how they work together, is key to making gel prints that look good. For harmonious, less busy prints consider analogous color. For combinations that clash rather than harmonize, consider complementary color combinations.

The Color Wheel

A color wheel is a chart that represents colors arranged according to their relationship. The basic color wheel consists of 12 colors that can be broken down into three groups: primary, secondary, and tertiary.

Primary colors are red, green, and blue, the primary colors of light–they cannot be made by mixing other colors. Primary colors sit equal distances apart on the color wheel and technically all other colors can be mixed from them. Some color blends are much more difficult than others and this is why you can purchase so many ready mixed paint colors!

Secondary colors are formed by mixing two primary colors in equal quantities–violet, green, and orange.

Tertiary colors are produced by an equal mixture of a primary color with a secondary color– yellow-green, blue-green, blue-violet, red-violet, red-orange, yellow-orange.

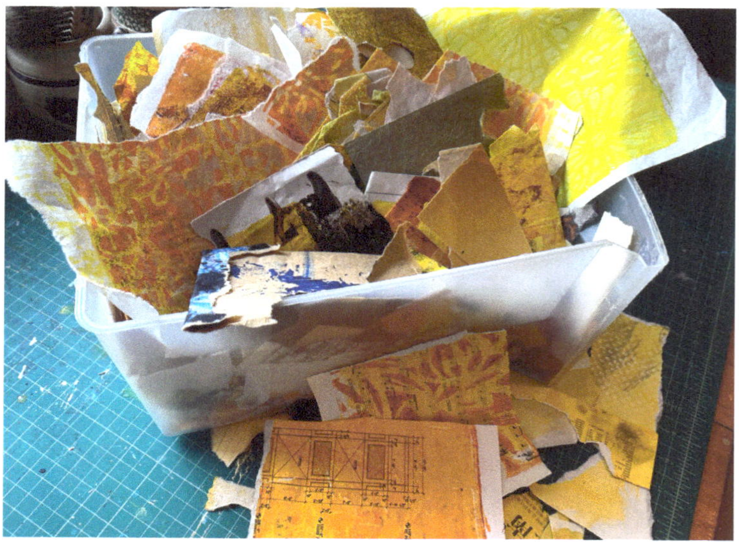
Yellow monoprints take advantage of analogous colors yellow, yellow-orange, and orange

Complementary colors are across the wheel from one and other–red and green, violet and yellow, orange and blue–these colors in combination create color discord.

Analogous colors are groups of three that are next to each other like blue, blue-green, and green–these colors in combination create color harmony.

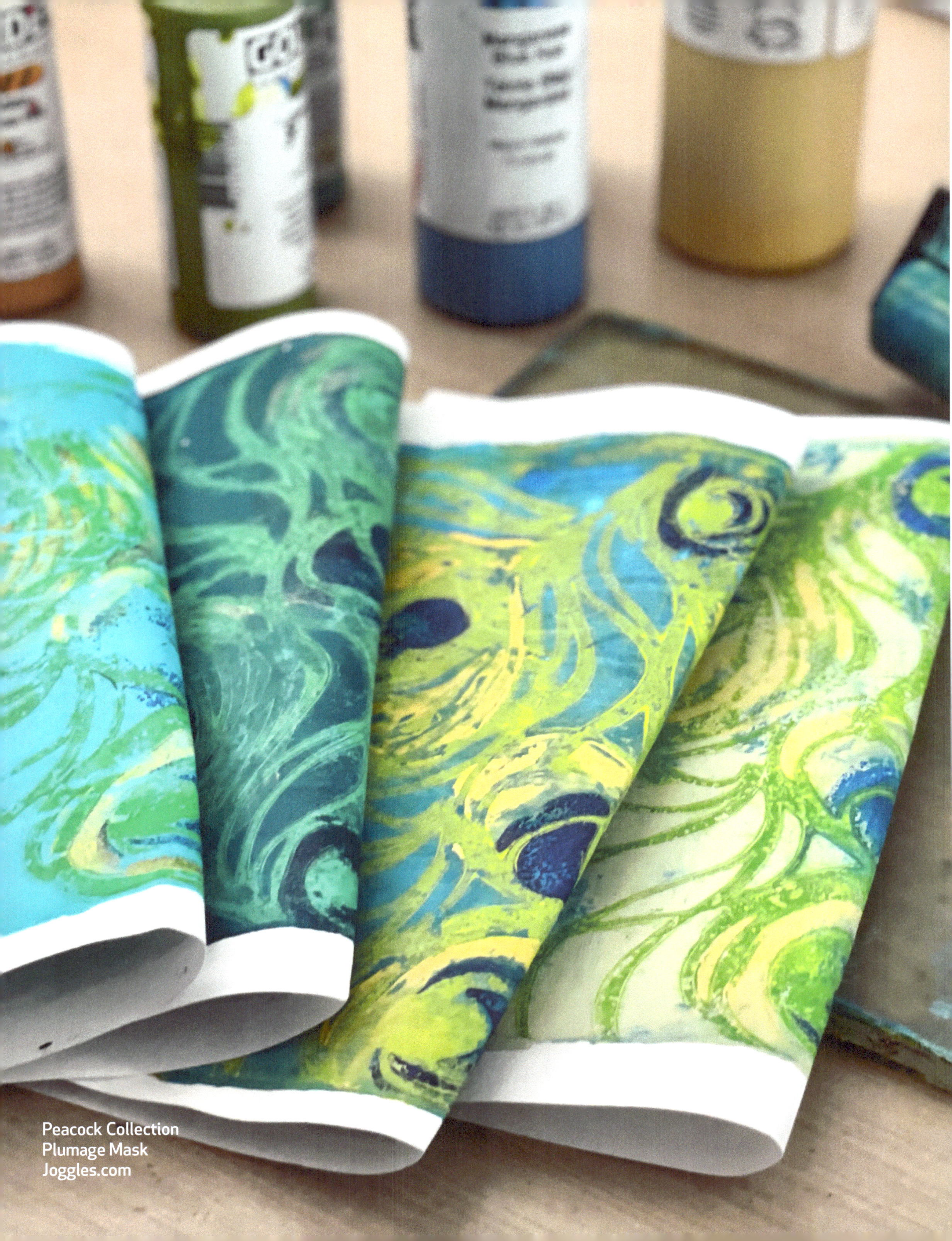
Peacock Collection
Plumage Mask
Joggles.com

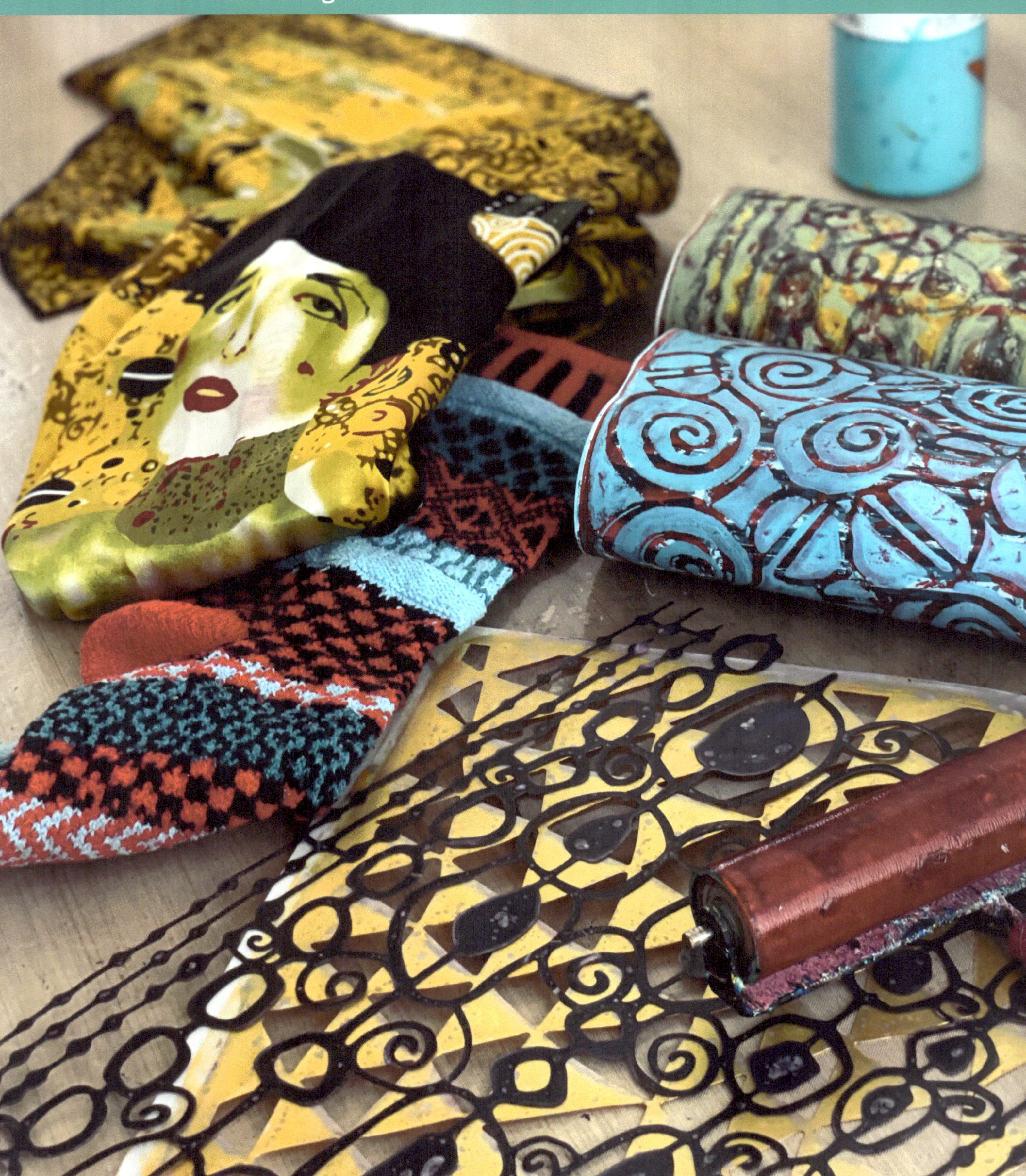

AMAZING GEL PRINTS: Working with Stencils

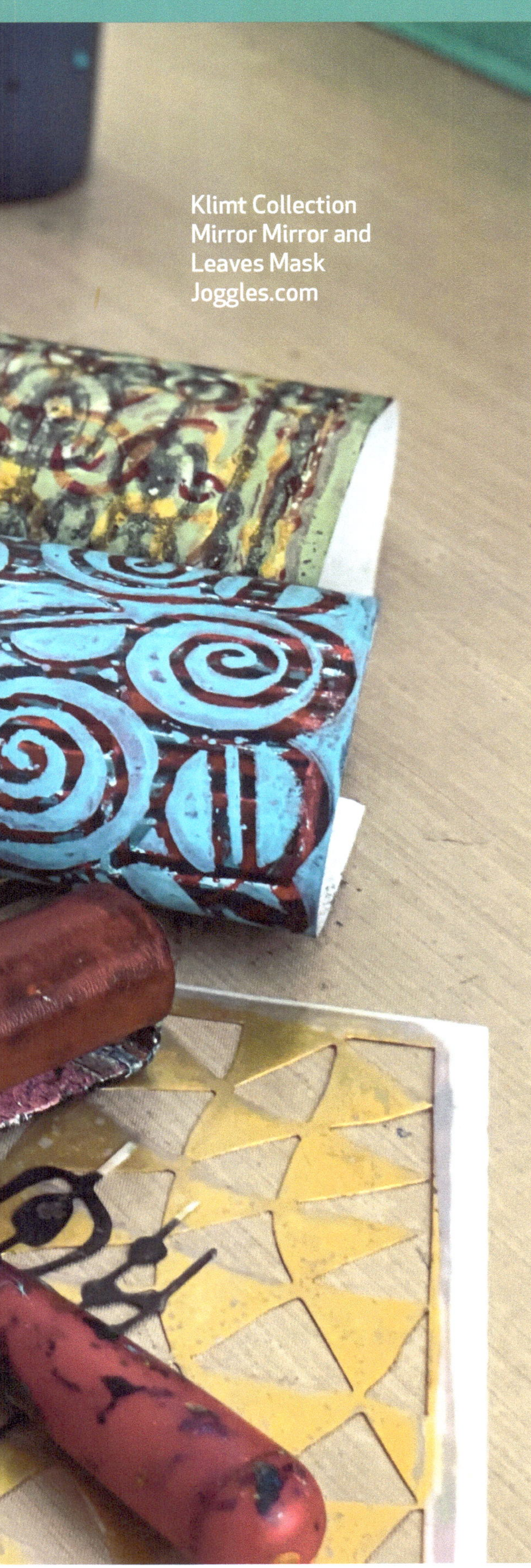

Color Combos

When you begin choosing color combinations, you might consider taking inspiration from the world around you. Look closely at color groupings in your clothes closet, your interior design, your linen closet, and your surroundings. Take photos of color combos that appeal to you when you are out and about and start building a library in your camera roll. It's very satisfying to begin your gel printing sessions with a plan for the colors you will use!

Inspired Color

For the prints on the left I pulled out a Gustav Klimt silk scarf and a Solemate sock, both in color combinations that appeal to me.

For the Klimt print I used Titan Green Pale, Quinacridone Red, Gold, and Paynes Gray Golden Fluid Acrylics–pulling my favorite colors from the scarf. I never use black in my gel printing, only dark values of deep colors, in this example the Paynes Gray served as my black.

For the sock print I used Cadmium Red, Teal, Titanium White, and Paynes Gray Golden Fluid Acrylics. I added Titanium White to the Teal in order to produce two values.

Titan Green Pale, Gold, and Teal are considered opaque colors, they will show up over darker layers and you can see that effect here especially with the teal in the sock print and the Titan Green Pale in the Klimt print.

In each of these prints I am utilizing TWO layered masks from my Gustav Klimt Collection.

COLOR COMBINATIONS

Starting with light colors and working your way down to darker colors is the way to go with Golden Fluid Acrylics, which are the paints I prefer in my process. Because most pigments are completely or partially translucent, a light color will not show up very well over a darker color (unless that light color is opaque). For this reason, I start light and every subsequent layer is a little darker. I also like to use colors that are next to each other on the color wheel for harmony, or colors that are across from each other for discord. I suggest experimenting with both to see what appeals to you.

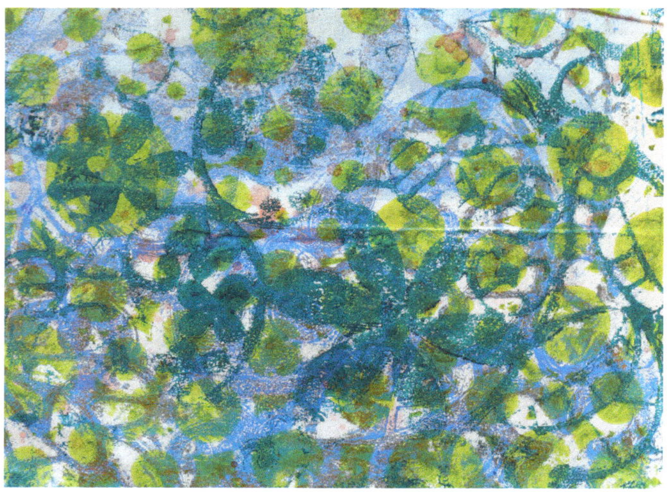

Analogous colors–starting with light blue green, to yellow green, to blue; creating color harmony

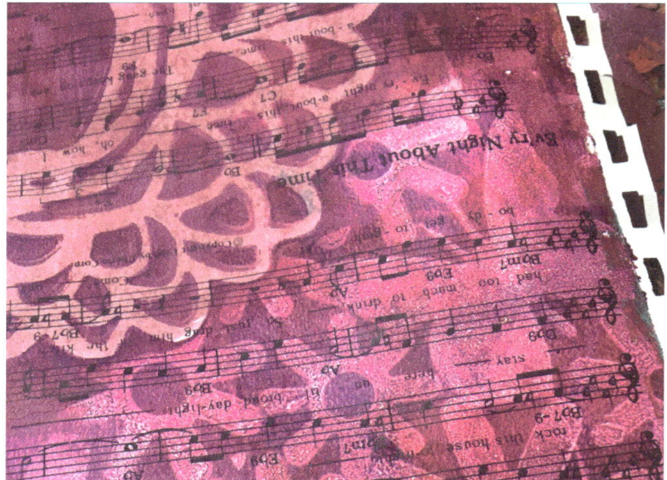

Analogous colors–starting with red violet, to violet, to blue violet; creating color harmony

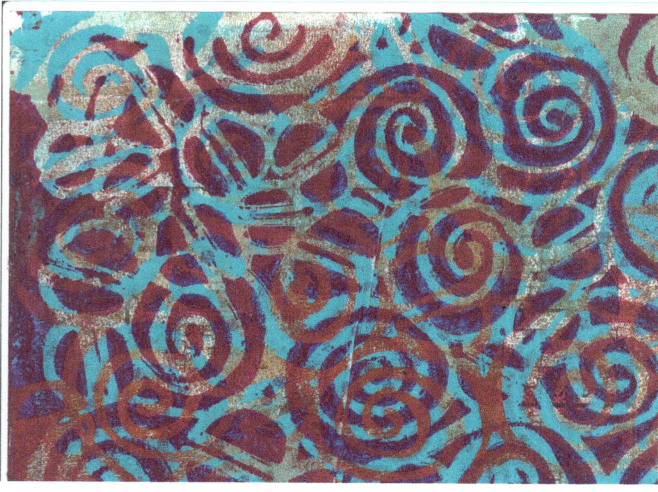

Complementary colors–starting with teal blue-green, to orange, to red violet; creating color discord

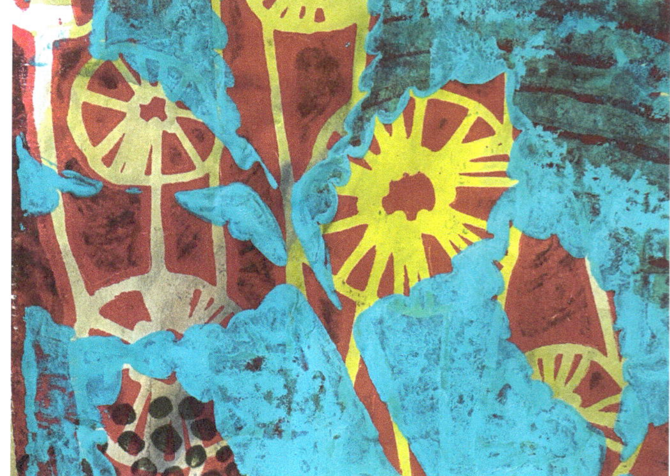

Complementary colors–starting with yellow green, to red, to teal blue-green (opaque); creating color discord

PIGMENT OPACITY

Layering colors on the gel plate requires an understanding of the opacity of pigments. Golden Fluid Acrylic packaging includes a hand-painted swatch of color over black tick marks on the label. This systems is not so much to demonstrate the color of the paint in the container, but rather to illustrate the opacity level of the pigment. If you can clearly see the black tick marks through the paint, it's highly translucent; if you can not see the black tick marks through the paint swatch at all, it's highly opaque. There are varying levels of opacity in pigments, using the color swatches on Golden's paint containers can help you to plan your gel printing layers.

Golden Fluid Acrylics are highly intense, permanent acrylic colors with a consistency similar to heavy cream. Produced from lightfast pigments, not dyes, they offer very strong colors with very thin consistencies.

Golden Paints have determined that an eight-point scale is most appropriate for describing the properties of their colors. They have assigned each color a number from 1 (most opaque) to 8 (most transparent) to indicate the opacity/transparency of that color. You can find this wealth of information on their website: GoldenPaints. com/TechnicalData/Pigment.

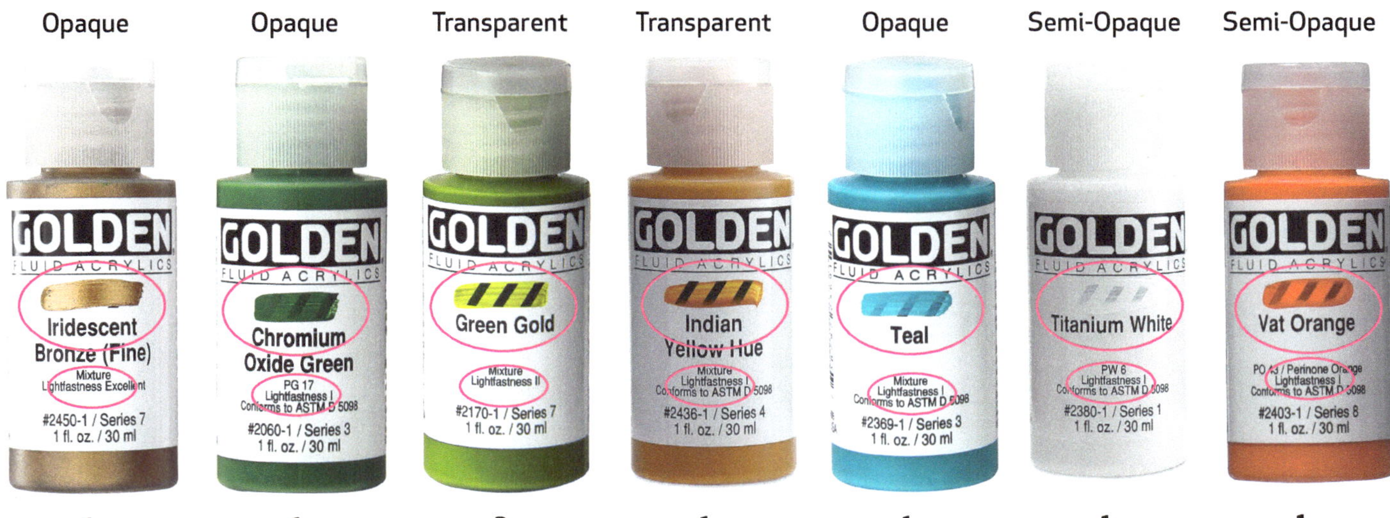

PIGMENT LIGHTFASTNESS

The Lightfastness Ratings are provided by the American Society for Testing and Materials. Colors with a Lightfastness Rating of I are considered Excellent and those with a Lightfastness Rating of II are Very Good. Color samples are exposed to an accelerated dose of light energy equivalent to that which would be expected to occur during approximately 100 years of museum-lit conditions. This exposure is condensed into approximately 15 weeks of testing time, or less, depending upon the accelerated test methods used. For

the purposes of the official test, before and after color difference is determined using a spectrophotometer, and difference units are mathematically calculated. Less than 4 units color change earns a color the designation of Lightfastness I. In practicality, this means that a visual comparison of the unexposed and exposed samples, when held adjacent, would reveal, at worse, a barely perceptible color change.

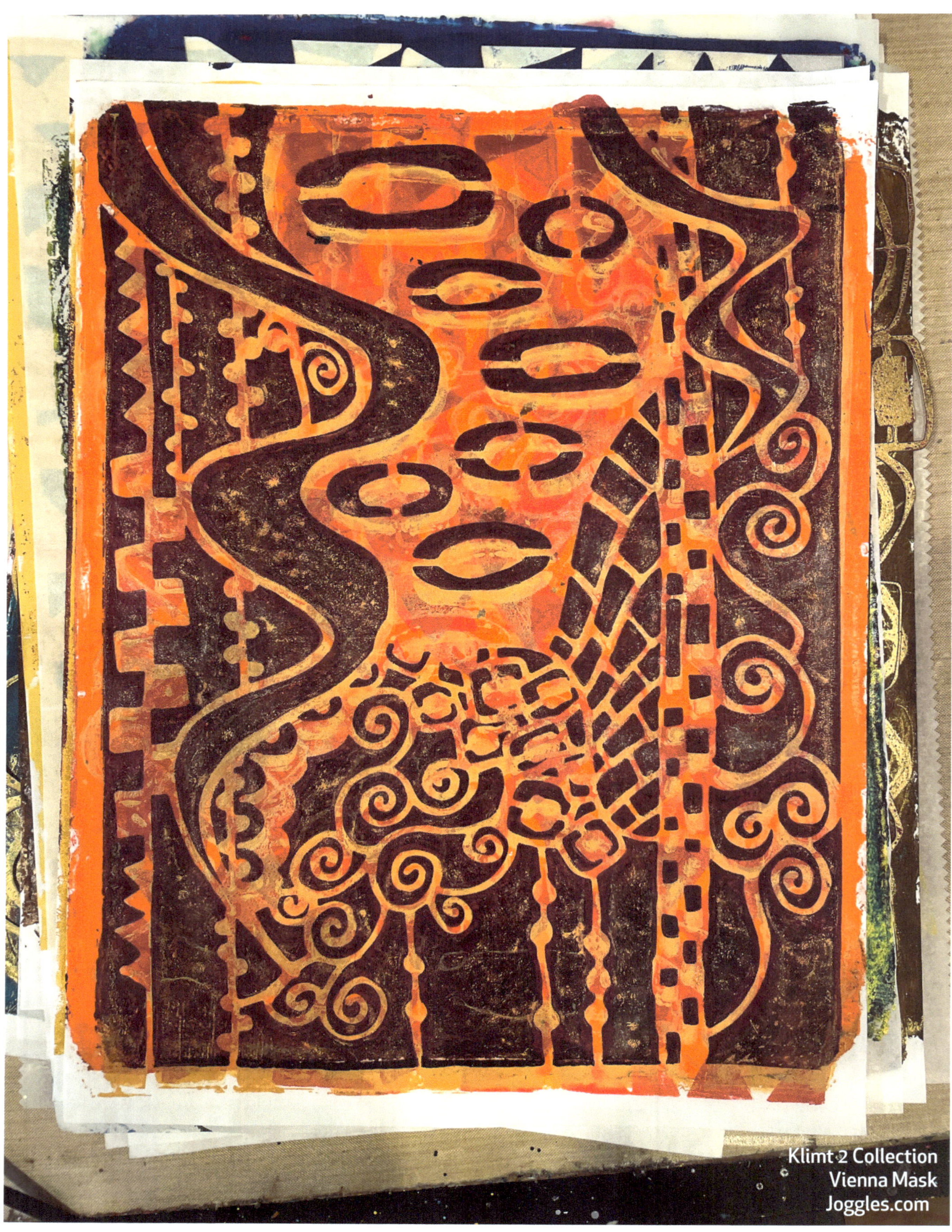

AMAZING GEL PRINTS: Working with Stencils

Permission to Play

They key to learning new techniques with the gel plate is experimentation. Most of the techniques presented in this book are a result of many hours of playing with the plate, the paints, and the stencils/masks. Some concepts have worked out better than others—some have yielded amazing results and some have been less than remarkable.

Often times, it's a happy accident that leads the way to a new technique, this is why giving yourself permission to play is so important. Take some time with your plate and stencils to experiment and see what happens.

Layering is key, the more layers you have the richer, deeper, more textural your prints will turn out. In order to achieve this you will always work from light to dark in your color application.

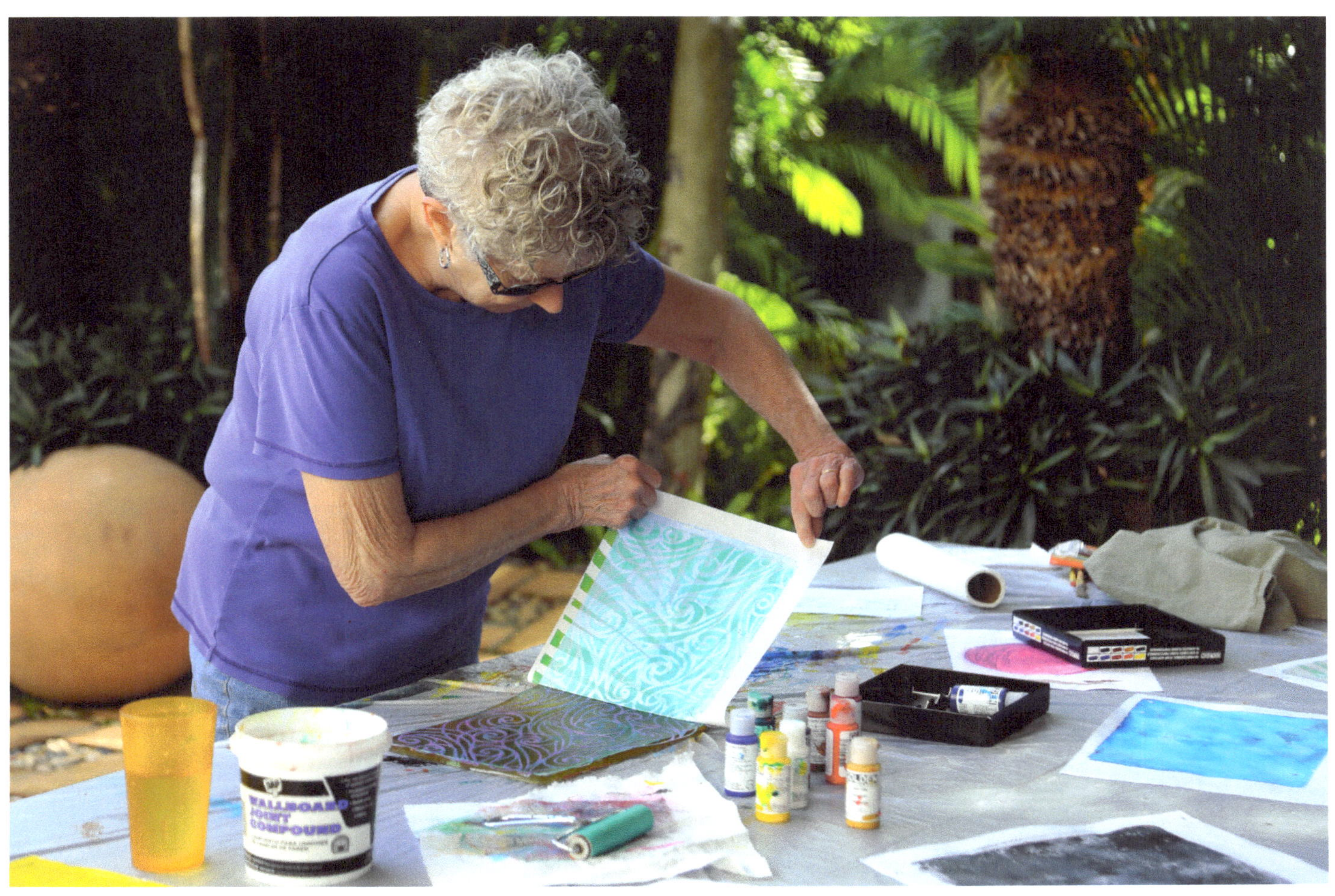

Stencils and Masks

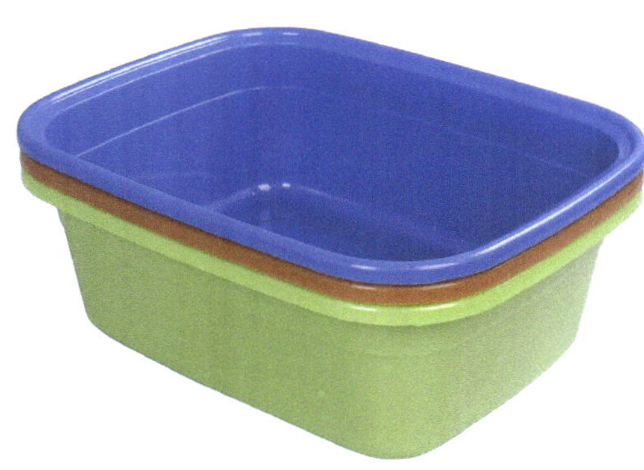

Stencils and masks offer hours of experimenting fun with your gel plate. I have designed many 9x12's with gel printing specifically in mind; I employ curvilinear shapes, organic patterns, and thin lines.

When the pattern is created by negative space (holes), that's a stencil. When the pattern is created by the positive space (mylar material), that's a mask. There are framed masks, where there is a border around the mylar pattern to keep it together, and there are some free-form masks that do not need a border. I design my stencils and masks for Joggles.com, a small family owned business located in Rhode Island, they are made in the USA.

In order to keep your stencils and masks clean, it's a good idea to have a dish basin full of soapy warm water on hand to toss your stencils (and other tools) in between usage. Keeping your stencils clean will help to preserve their longevity by keeping the very small detailed areas from filling in with acrylic paint–this can eventually ruin the stencil.

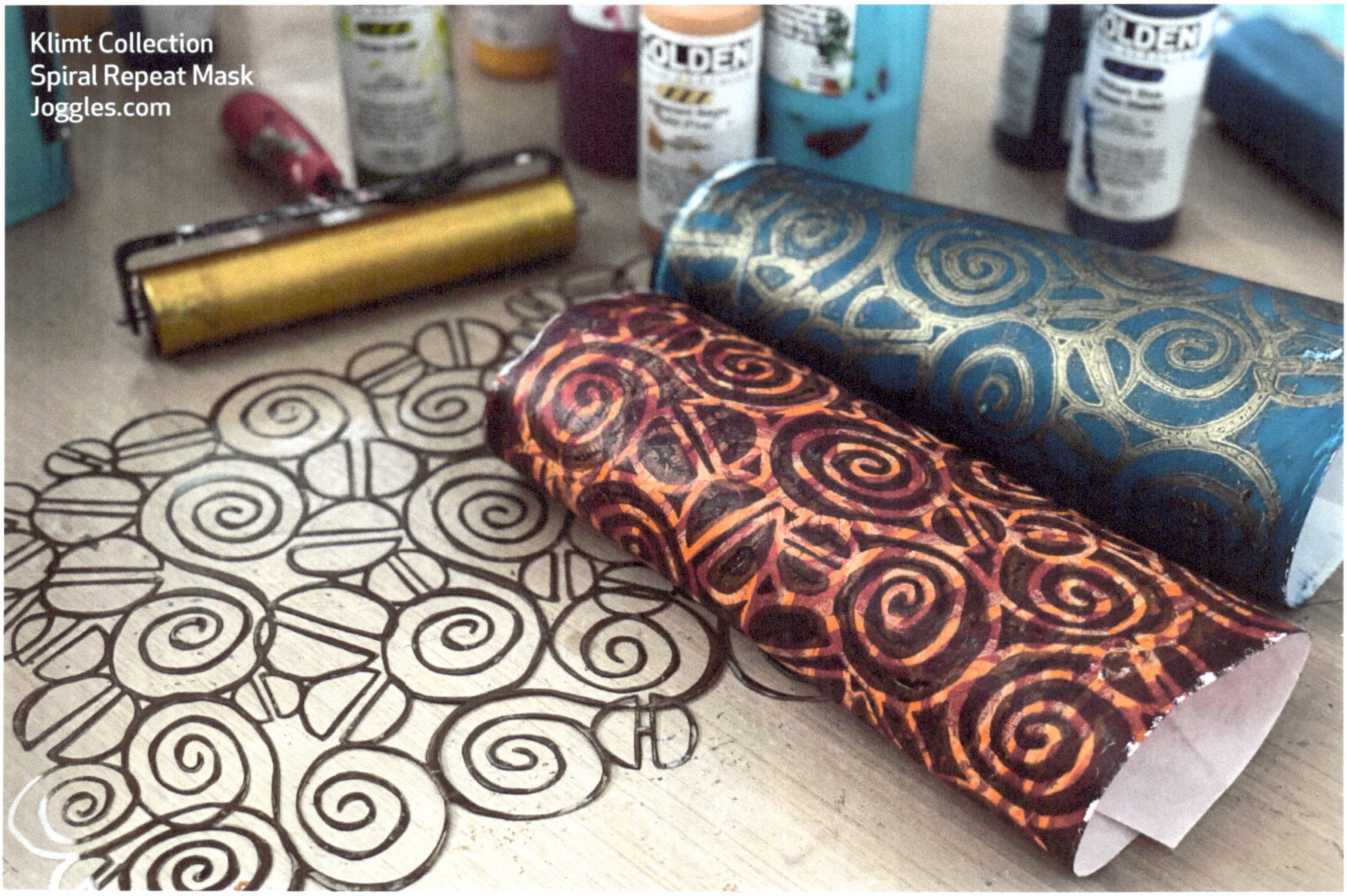

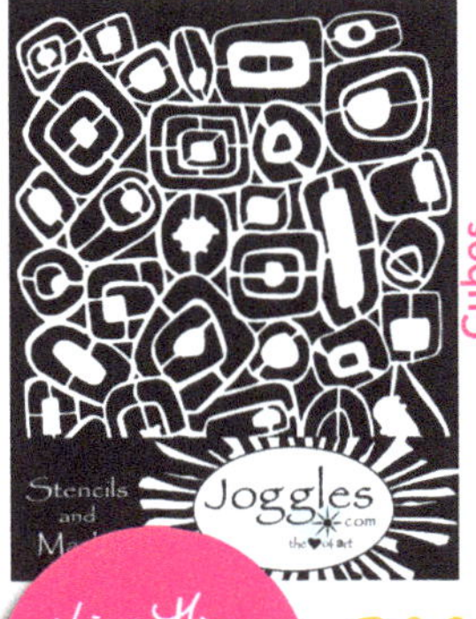

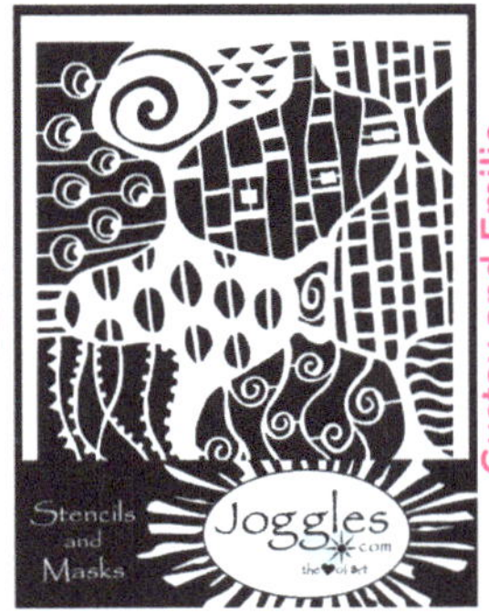

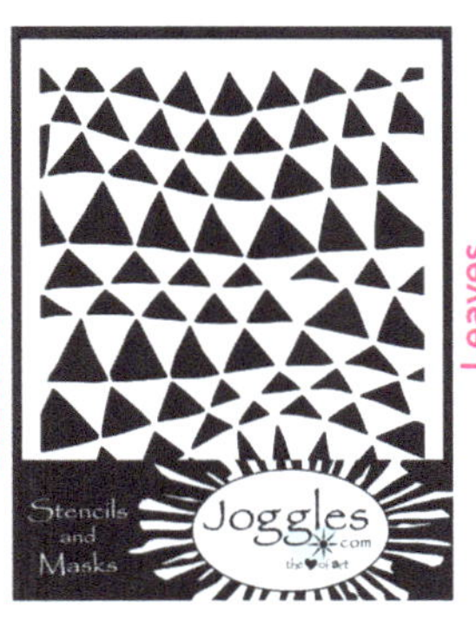

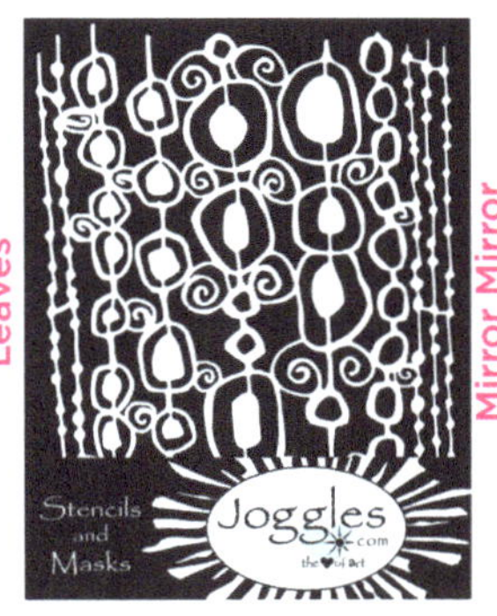

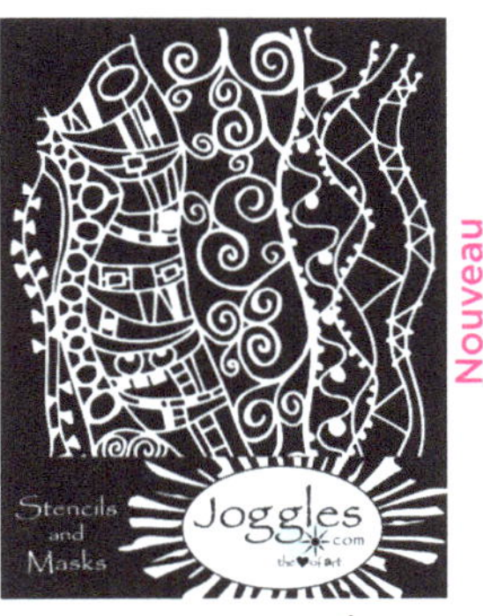

GUSTAV KLIMT INSPIRED

STENCILS and MASKS

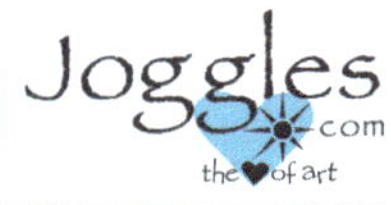

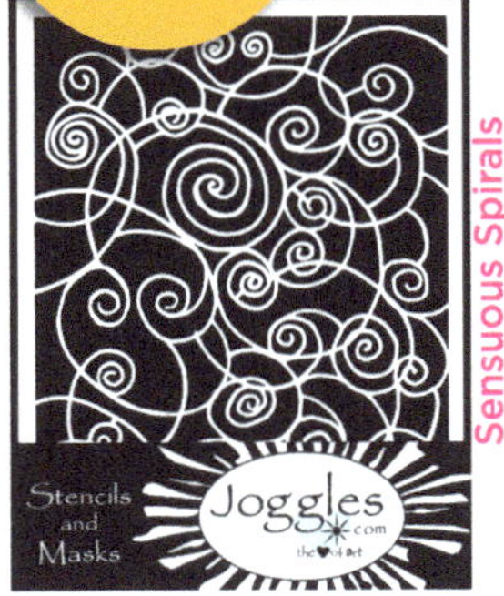

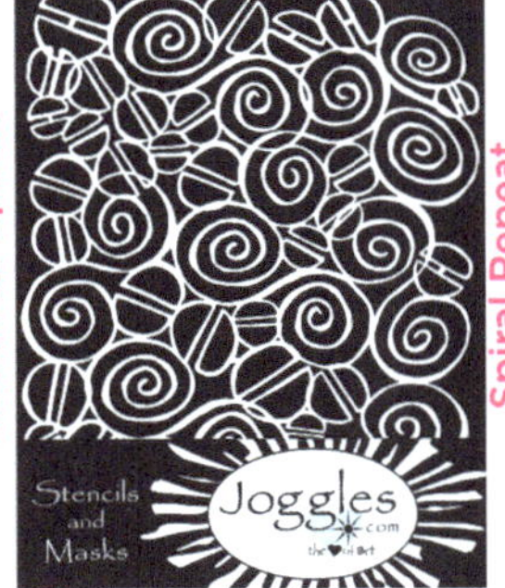

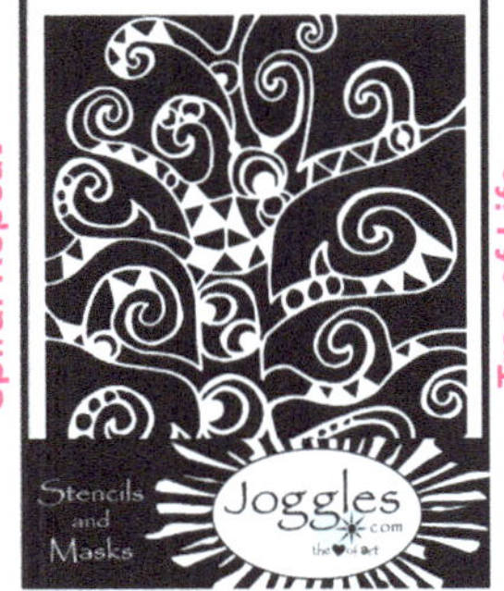

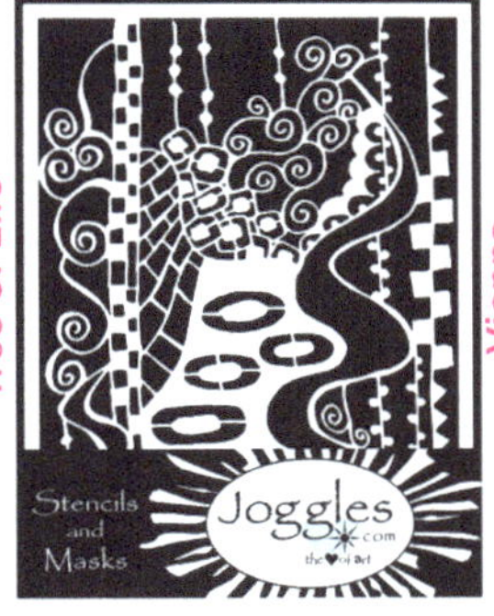

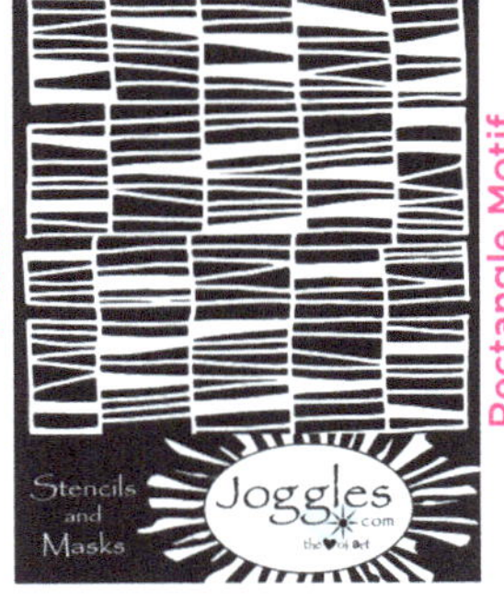

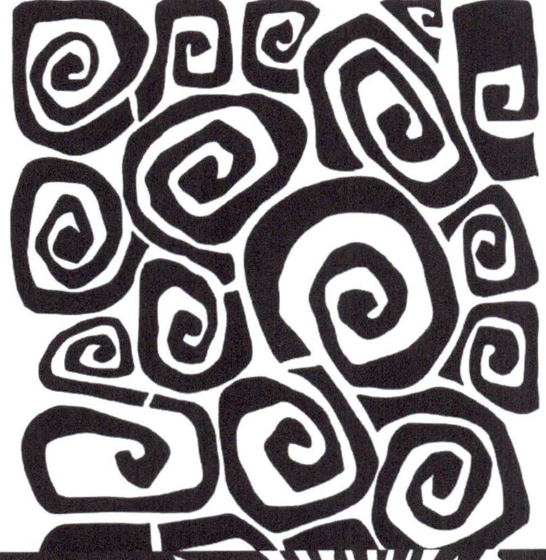

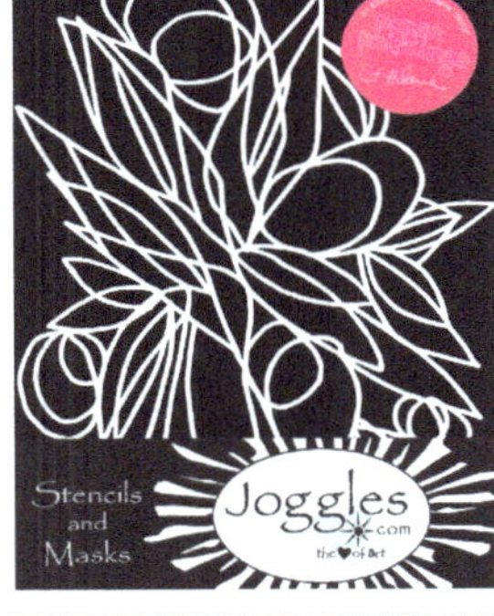

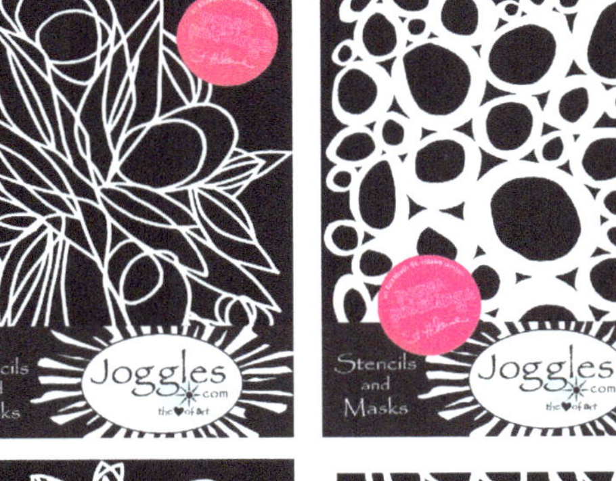

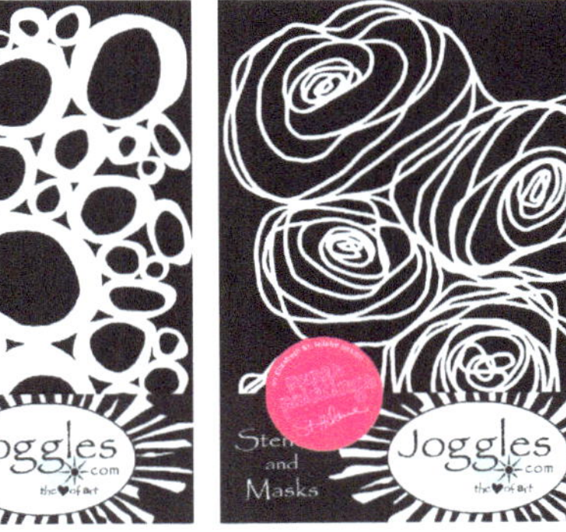

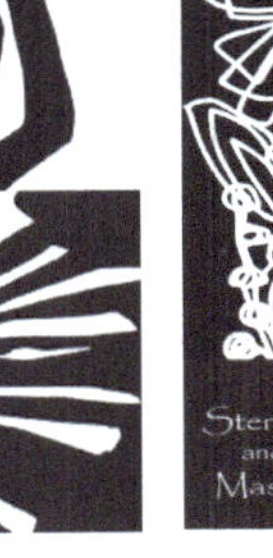

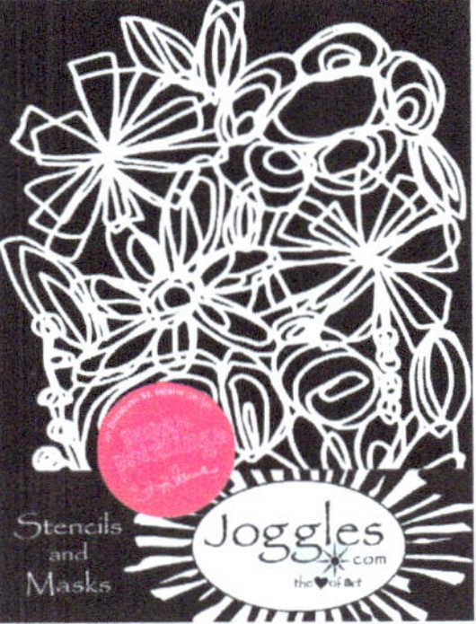

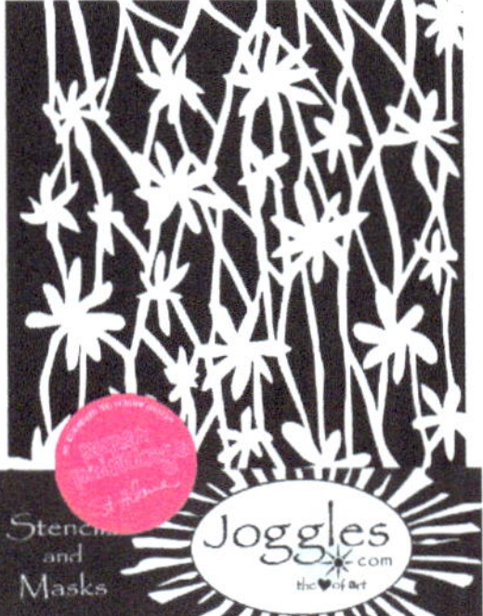

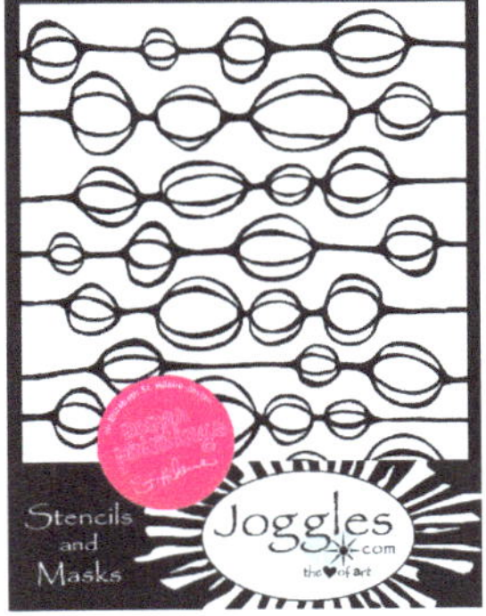

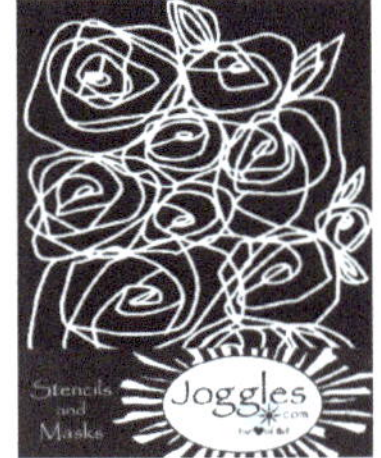

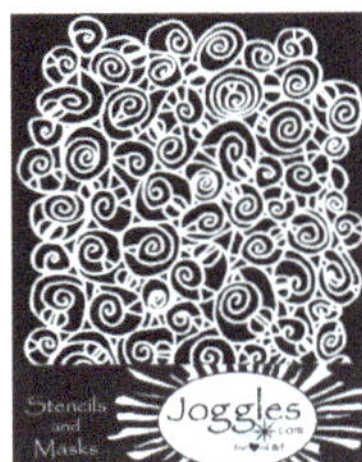

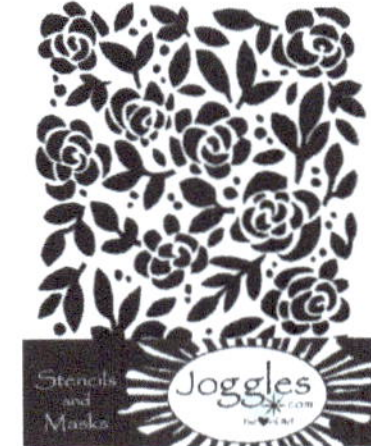

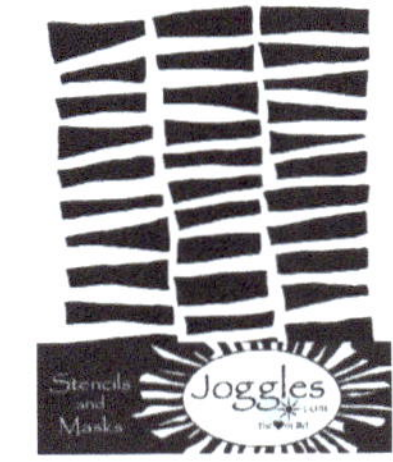

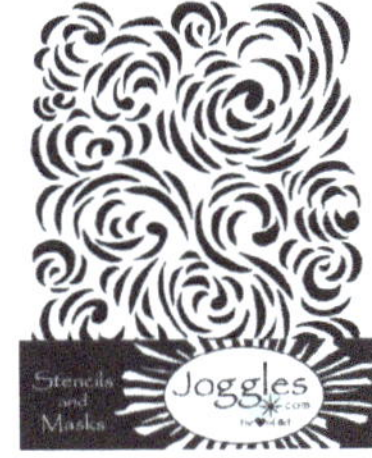

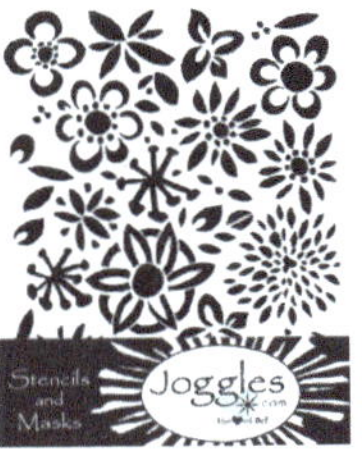

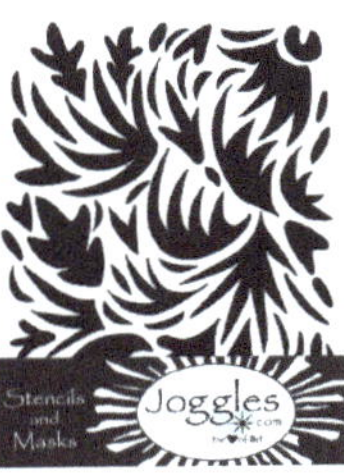

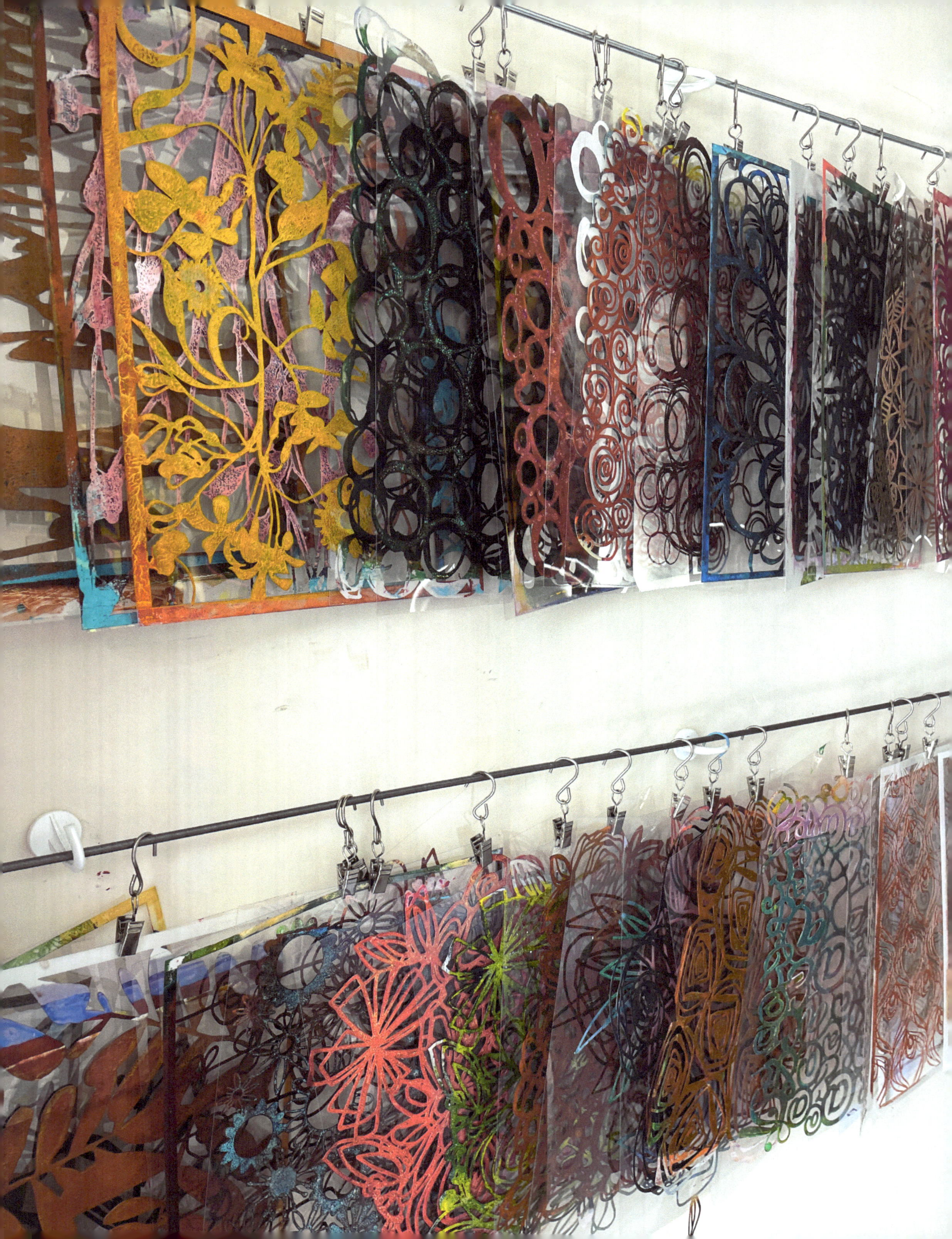

Storage Solutions

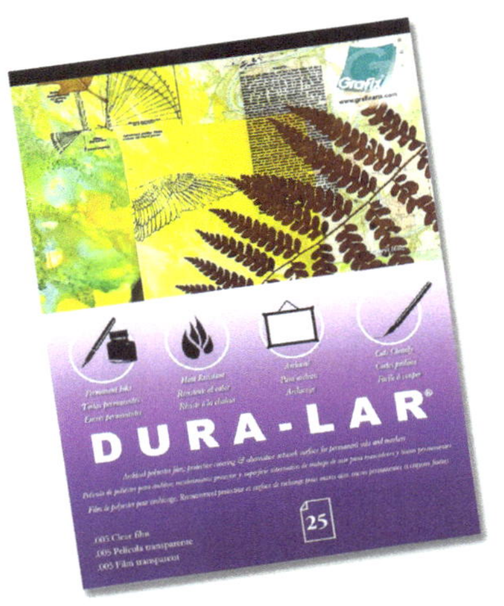

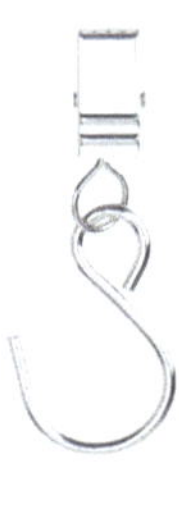

Stencils and masks should be stored in a manner that keeps them from tangling and allows them to remain easily viewed. Layering them between sheets of solid paper in a drawer keeps them from tangling, but doesn't help you to know what you have at a quick glance.

A system that I have implemented that works for me is to hang them slightly overlapping on a metal dowel with swivel clips and sheets of clear Dura-Lar plastic sheets in between. This system not only keeps them from tangling but it also helps me to be able to evaluate what I have and what I want to use at a glance.

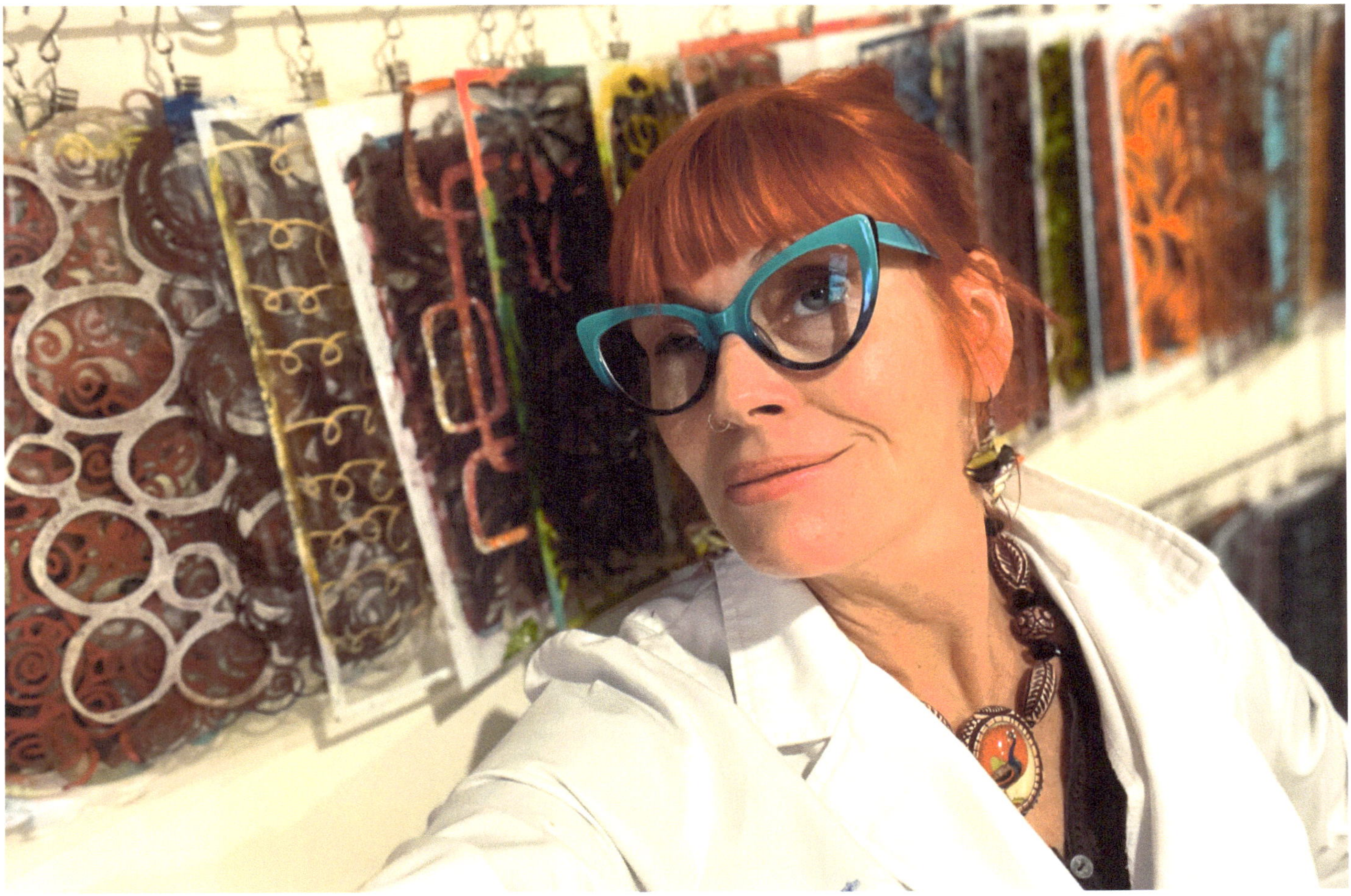

Gel Plate

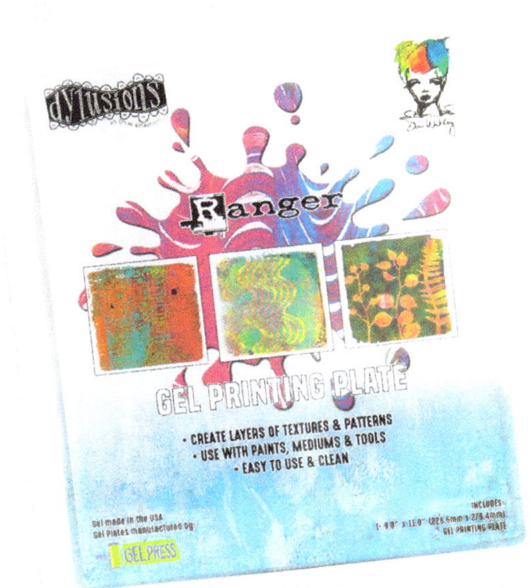

There are many brands and sizes of gel plates available commercially. I have plates in every size from 5x7 for printing cards to 12x14 for making collage paper. When using my 9x12 stencils and masks however, the 9x12 gel plate is the one I find to be the best. I prefer this plate because it allows me to use the full stencil/mask design area, especially when combined with my favorite 9x12 pad of Sumie-E Sketch rice paper–it's the perfect combination!

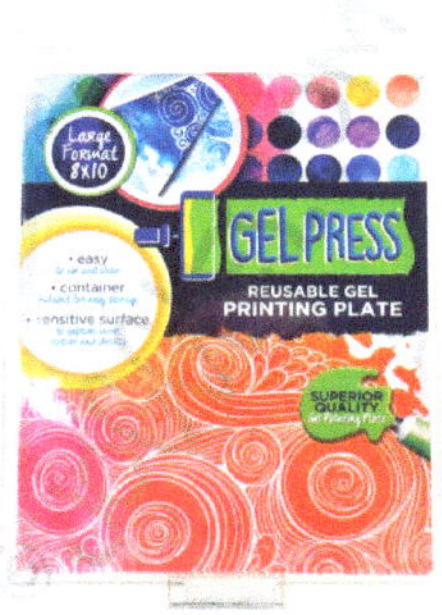

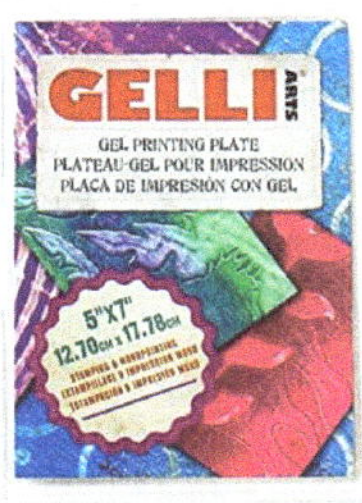

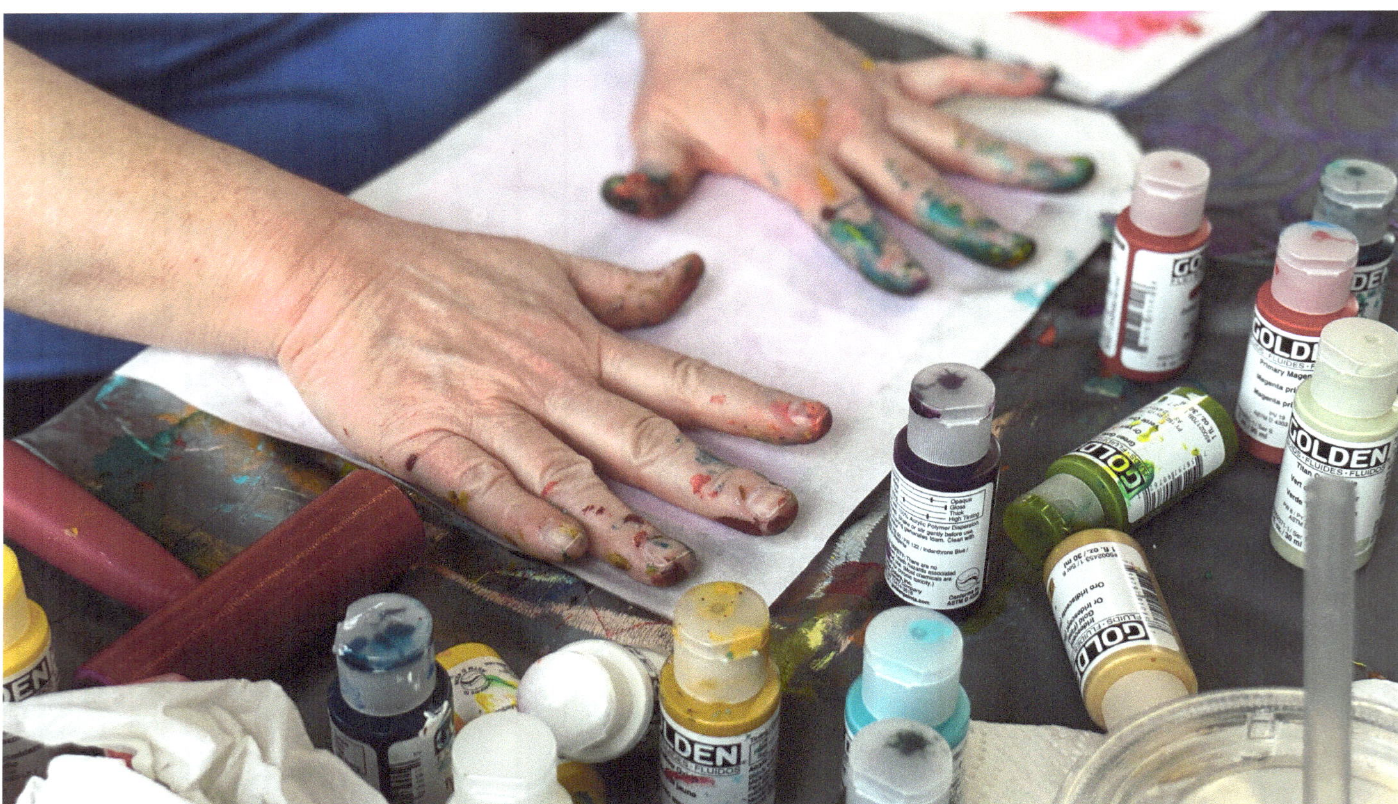

Gel plates come in a wide variety of sizes and brand names

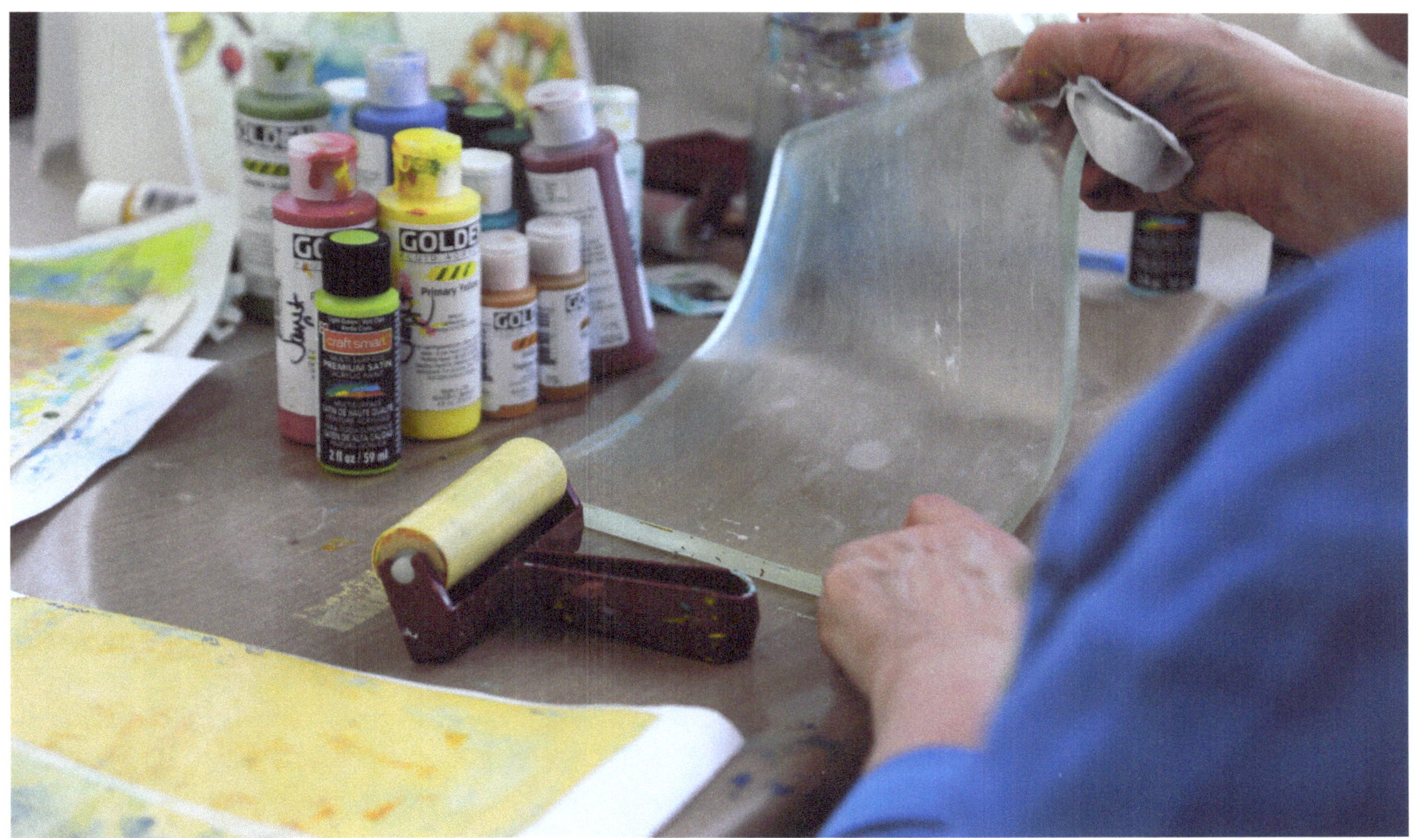

Set your brayer down on the back edge, facing up. This way it will not stick to your work surface as the paint dries.

Brayers

Brayers are used to apply a thin layer of paint to your plate. There are a wide variety of brayers quality and price. I have some super expensive print-making brayers that are like BUTTER and I have some el-cheapo plastic brayers that are, well... El cheapo.

You'll have to go with what your budget allows, I have found Speedball to make brayers that do not break the bank but are significantly higher quality than the plastic ones I have used.

I like to use the Speedball six-inch deluxe soft rubber brayer because I can cover the plate with paint in a few strokes. I also like to use a two inch hard rubber brayer for applying paint in smaller, more specific areas. To be completely indulgent, I use two brayers, one for warm and one for cool colors. This

setup is very helpful in preventing opposite color contamination, allowing me to switch colors without worrying about getting the brayer completely clean.

The best way clean your brayer is to roll it off onto a clean sheet of paper. That sheet of clean up paper will eventually work as a base layer for some interesting gel printing, so don't throw it away. I roll excess paint from my brayer onto the pages of an old book.

Always set the brayer on the back edge so that the roller is facing up, this way it will not stick or transfer paint to your work table .

AMAZING GEL PRINTS: Working with Stencils

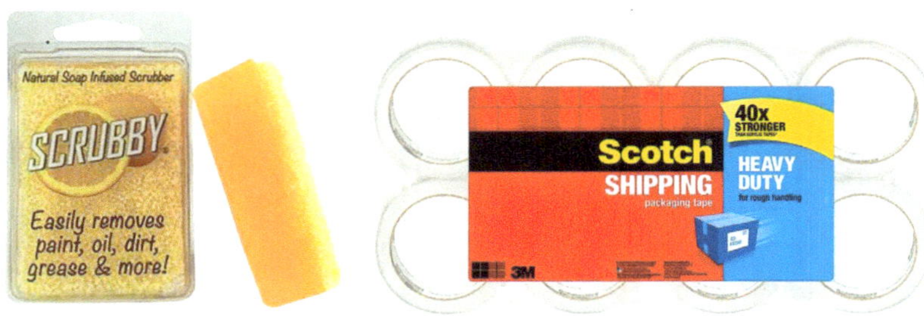

CLEANING YOUR PLATE

You will find a lot of in information on the Internet about cleaning your gel plate. Some will suggest baby wipes, others will suggest mineral oil, scrubbing, or soaking.

I have found that using heavy duty Scotch shipping tape (I buy it by the eight-pack) is the best way to peel all paint off the plate that you do not get off with a rice paper pad print (the Sumie-E 9x12 Sketch Pad pulls most of the paint from your plate).

If your last print has not removed all the paint, wait for the plate to be totally dry, strip the tape over the entire surface, rub it down hard, and then peel it back! So easy, and satisfying as it peels all the dried paint away from the surface of the gel plate.

When I get paper stuck to my plate, I find the best way to get that off is to run it under water and gently scrub it with the Scrubby soap bar that has mild glycerin citrus soap and a gentle scrubbing surface–this product works great on your hands too!

STORING YOUR PLATE

Remove the mylar sheets on both sides of the plate, these are part of the manufacturing process and are meant to be discarded.

Keep your plate in the plastic clamshell packaging it shipped in, and store it on the shelf like a book. Do not stack things on top of your gel plate, this will cause bubbles to form in it.

If your clamshell eventually becomes damaged, Ranger manufactures gel press storage tins in many sizes. If you have smaller gel plates of various sizes, you can consolidate them into a single tin, this saves shelf space.

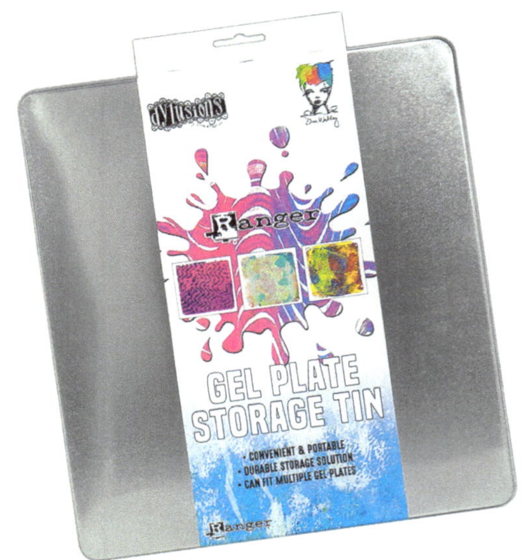

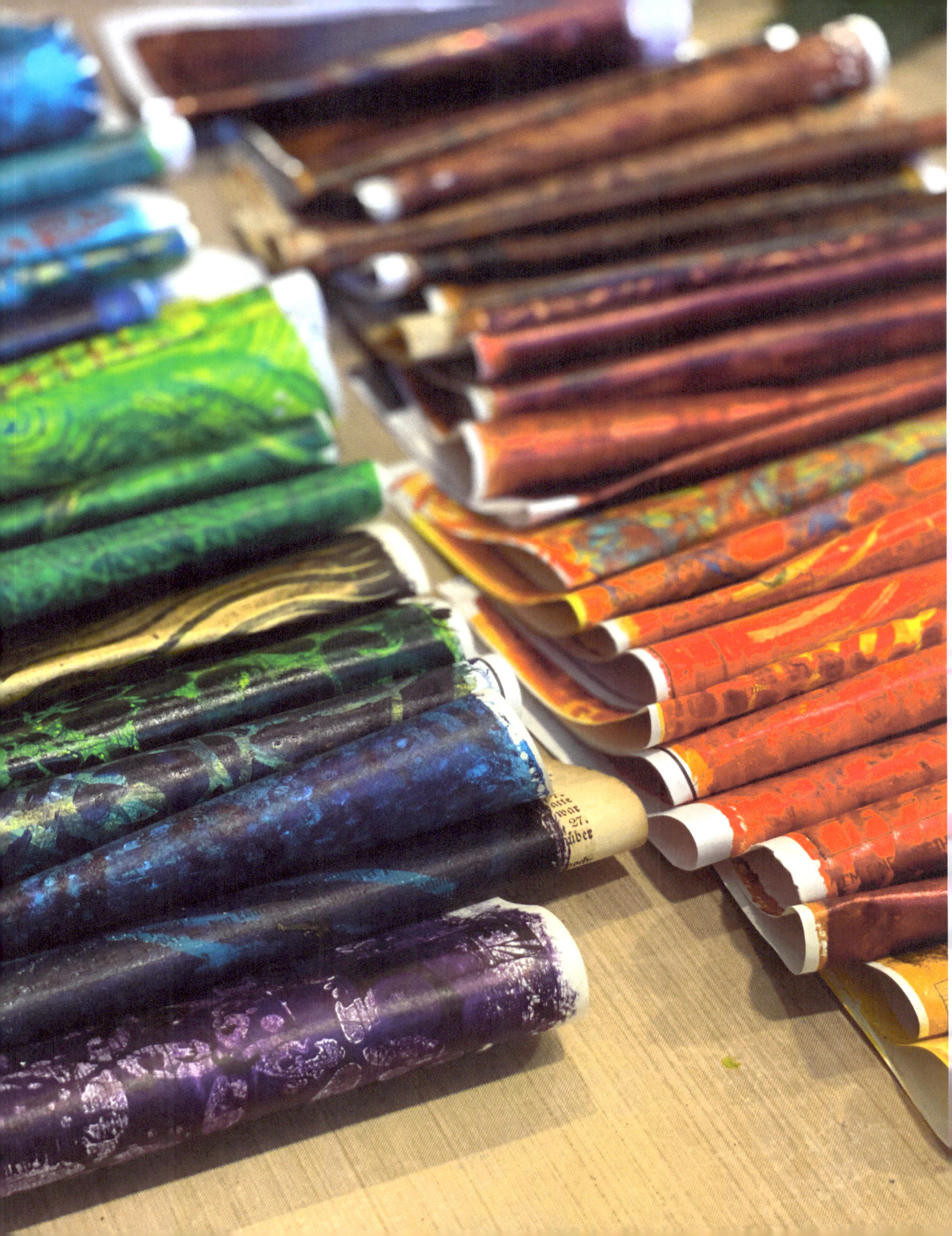

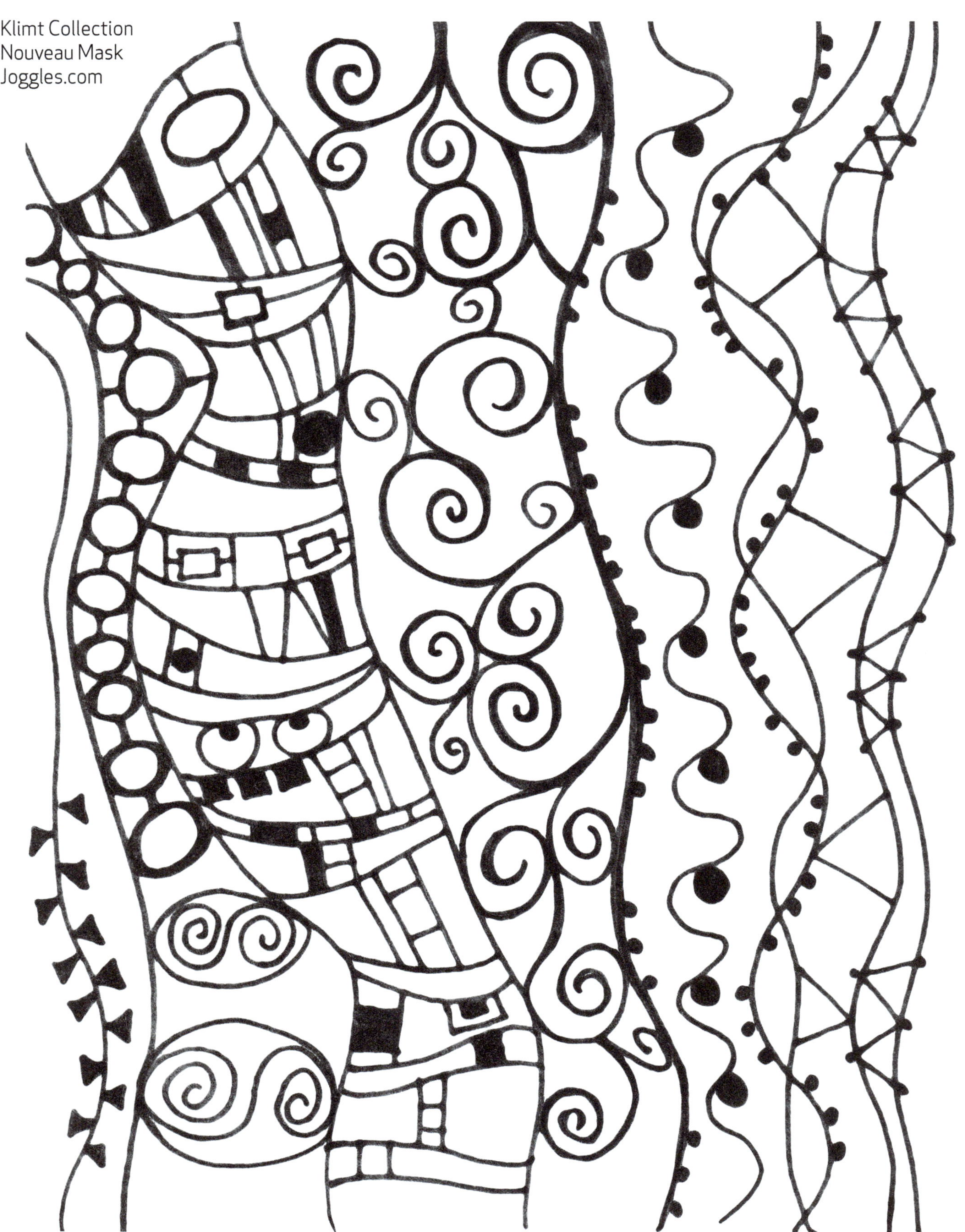
Klimt Collection
Nouveau Mask
Joggles.com

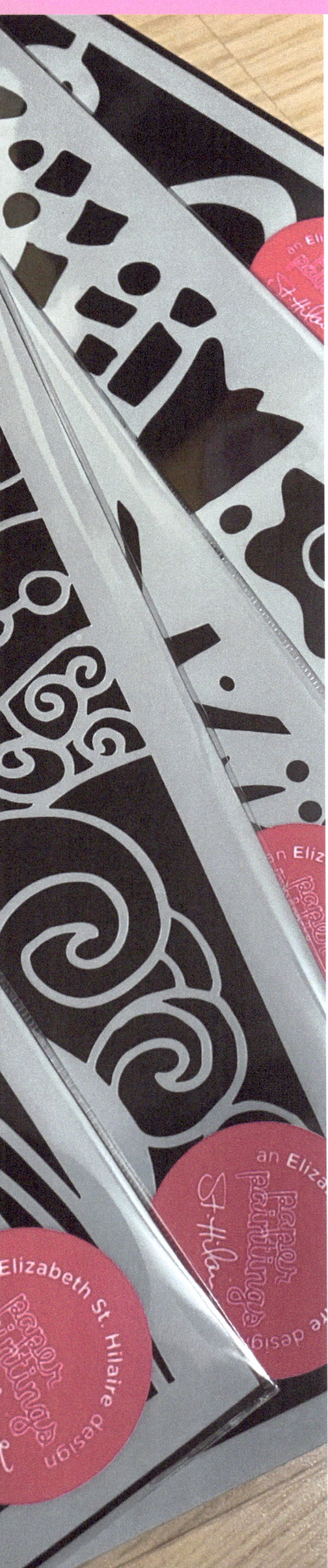

CHAPTER

2 Jumping In!

Choosing quality stencils and masks that are laser cut with fine line detail will produce the most interesting and beautiful prints. On the left is one of my many 9x12" designs with Joggles.com, created specifically for layering on the gel printing plate.

Starting with light colors and working your way down to darker colors is the way to go for successful layering. Because Golden Fluid Acrylics are translucent, a light color will not show up very well over a darker color. For this reason, I start light and in every subsequent layer I go a little darker. I also like to use colors that are next to each other on the color wheel for harmony, or colors that are across from each other for discord. I suggest experimenting with both to see what appeals to you.

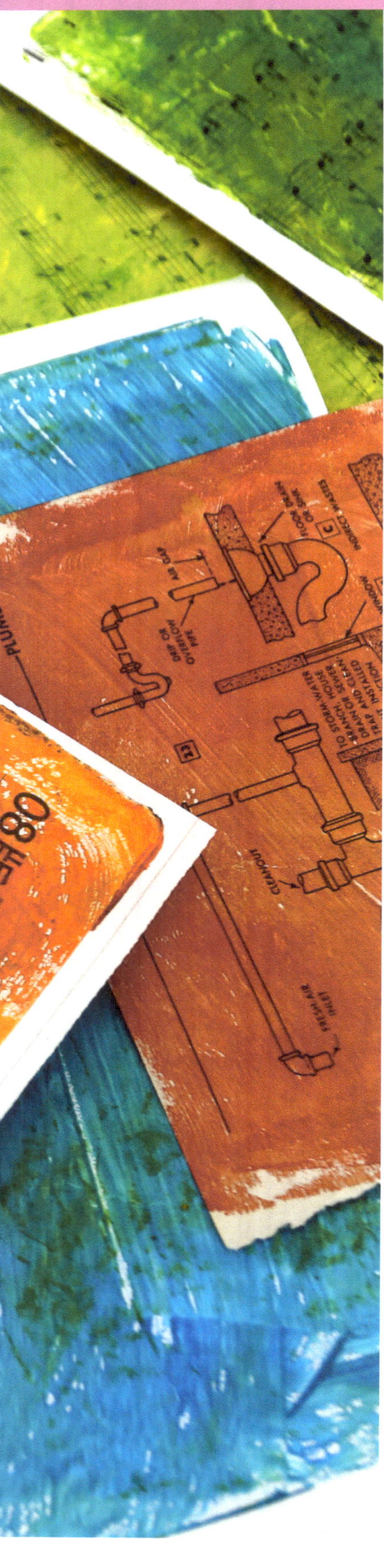

STARTING WITH

Light Colored Solids

The idea behind starting with a light colored base layer is that your prints don't include the white of the paper, which offers high contrast and can appear busy–high contrast can be distracting. Apple red paper should be layers of rich reds and intense oranges; adding white to this palette would be distracting.

In order to eliminate the whites, I always start with a solid base layer. I do not clean my plate between layers, this makes use of any residual paint on the plate from layer to layer. I call the leftover dried paint the crust. Your subsequent layers pick up the crust along with the newly applied paint–this creates often unexpected and beautiful results.

Start with the lightest value of the color you intend to make your print, in other words if your print is going to be green, use the lightest value of green that you have so that you can build subsequent layers of green and get gradually darker. My lightest green is typically Golden Fluid Acrylics Green Gold. This is a yellow-green that is very light and makes an excellent base for subsequent layers of green. Make yourself a few sheets of the lightest color of each set of analogous colors on the color wheel.

CREATING A SOLID BASE LAYER

Start by squeezing out a few drops of Golden Fluid Acrylics onto the plate and spreading it into a thin layer with the brayer. If your brayer is slipping and sliding across the plate, there is probably too much paint. If your brayer is removing the paint when you roll over it, then you probably need more paint. It takes a few test prints to get the hang of it.; Luckily you are making solid colors!

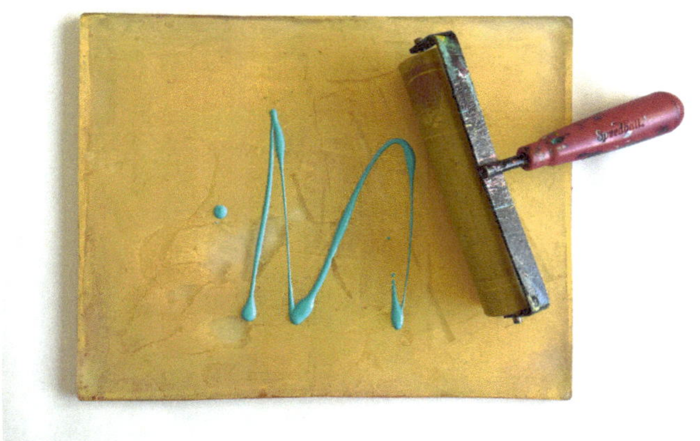

The brayer gives thin, even coverage for a few drops of paint (Teal) applied directly to the plate.

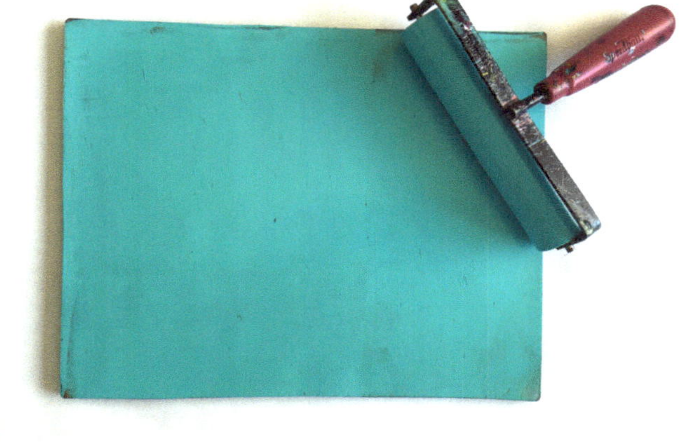

Roll the paint out thin, to evenly cover the surface of the plate with the brayer.

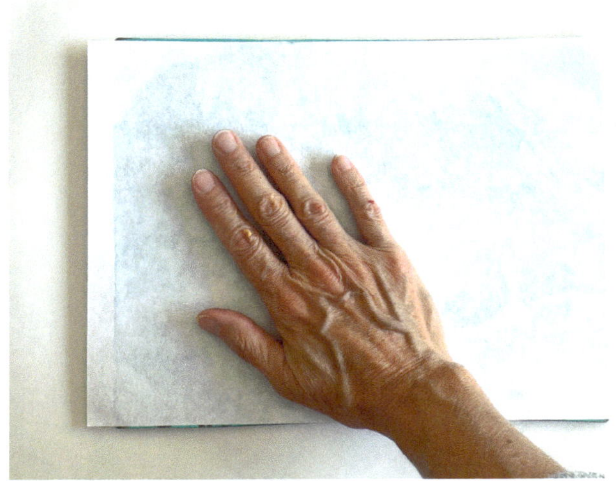

Press your chosen paper into the surface of the plate.

Pull the print.

EXAMPLES

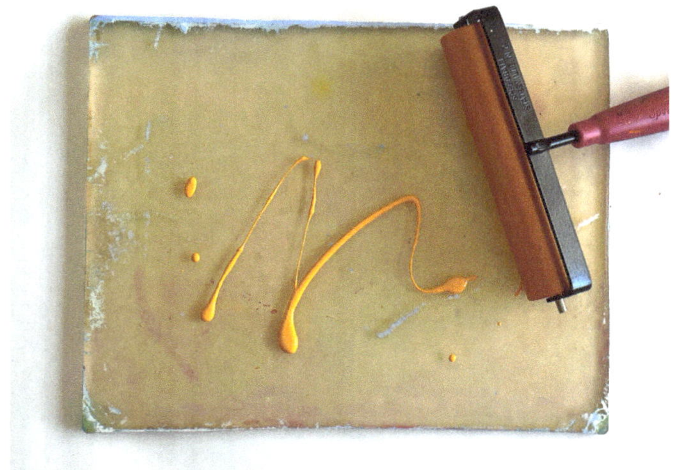

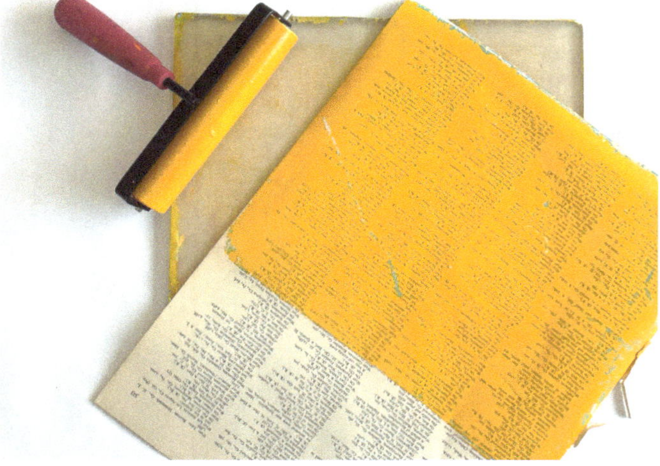

Diarylide Yellow

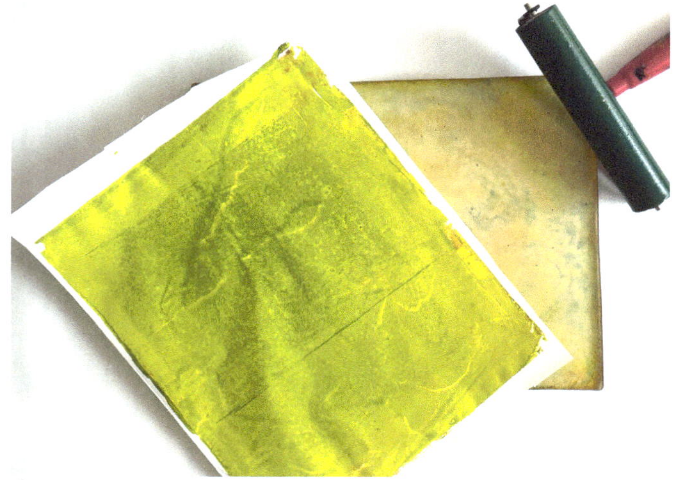

Green Gold

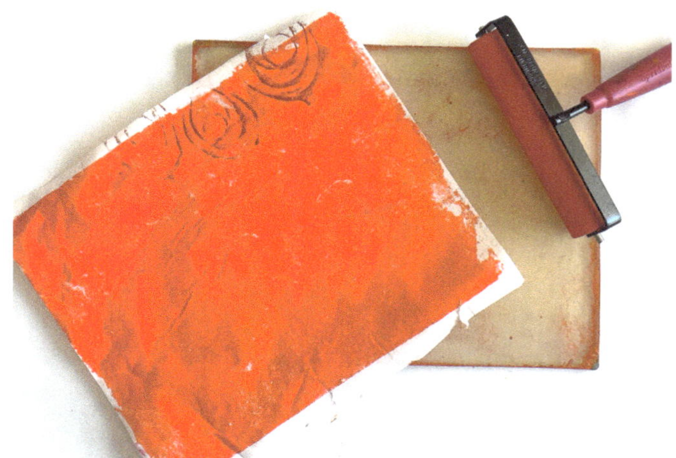

Pyrolle Orange

Quinacridone Nickle Azo Gold

If you want to create a deep, dark paper, you may want to start with a medium value and then apply darker layers down to a rich, deep value. Deep values of purple or rich blue paper can also be substituted for black in collage–I never paint black paper.

You may also like to incorporate metallics and opaque layers at the end as they stand out over dark due to their lack of translucency. Try blending metallics and opaque paints together with your base color, this will create nice harmony.

AMAZING GEL PRINTS: Working with Stencils

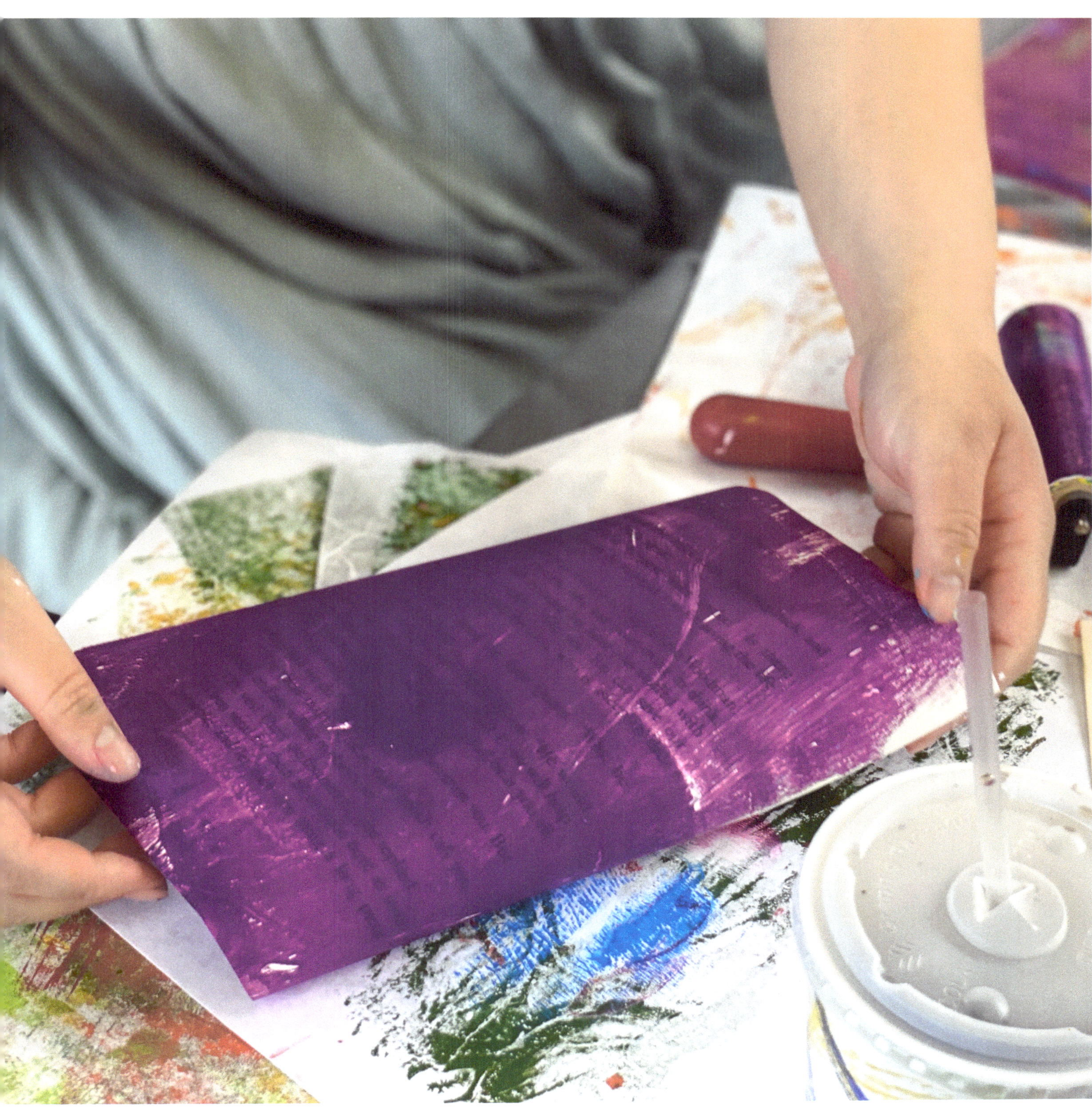

Permanent Violet Dark

AMAZING GEL PRINTS: Working with Stencils

BEGINNING WITH

Stencils and Masks

A stencil print offers immediate gratification, and who doesn't love that? The 9x12" mask covers your whole gel plate and even after just one layer, the prints are enough to make you giddy!

Over the years I have learned what I liked and didn't' like about the stencils that were commercially available. Recently I started designing my own line of stencils and masks with Joggles.com–putting my teaching and gel printing experience to the test in order to help me to design for effects I wanted.

After you have gotten your light colored solids ready, the next step is to make a straight forward stencil/mask print on top. Remember to work from light to dark, each layer should be just a wee bit darker than the one before in order for you to employ several layers before the whole sheet gets too dark.

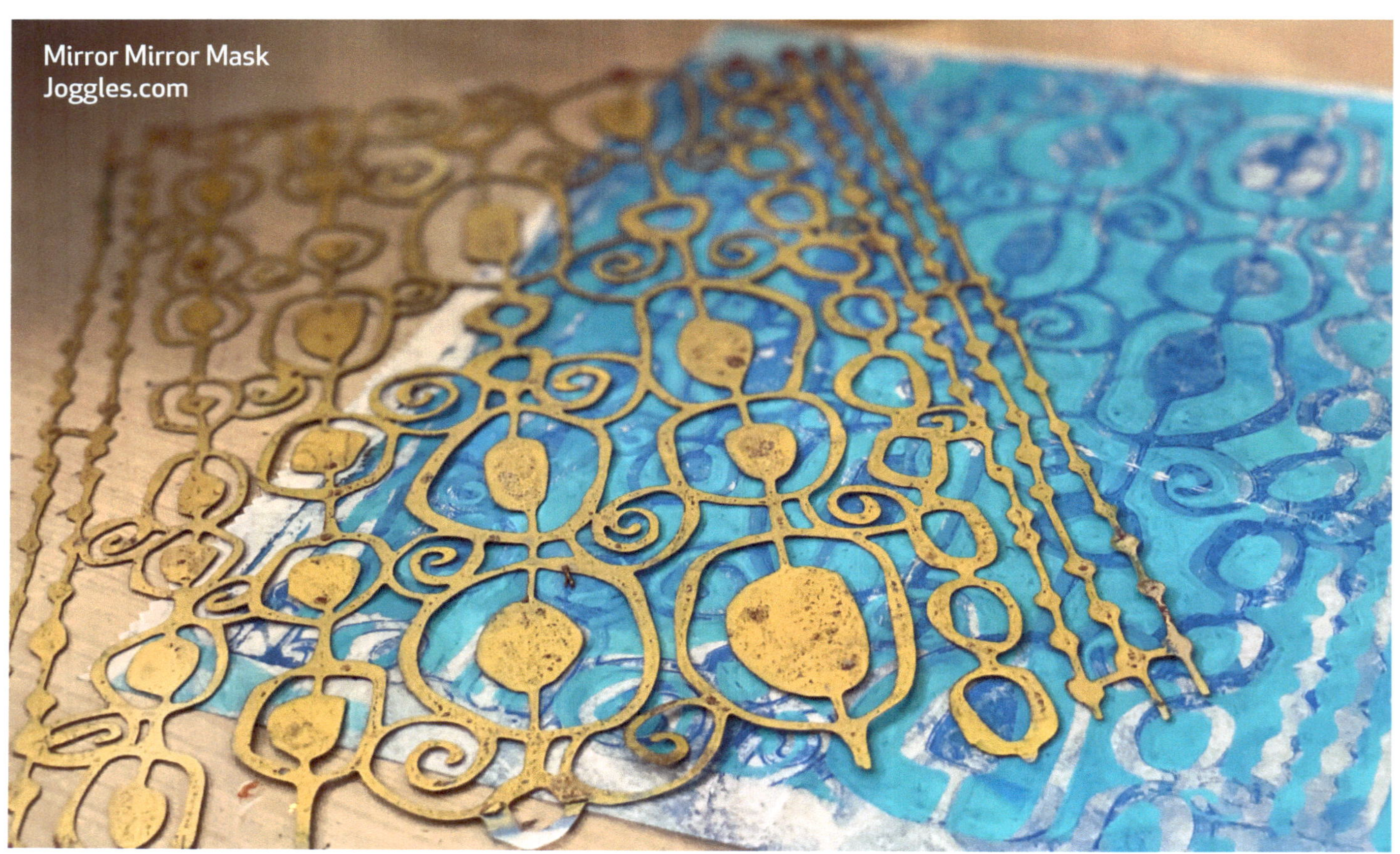

THE BASICS

The process of making light colored solids helped you master the amount of paint to use, handling the brayer, working with different types of paper, and getting the hang of the overall process. Now it's time to try your hand at stencils and masks, practicing layering patterns and combining colors.

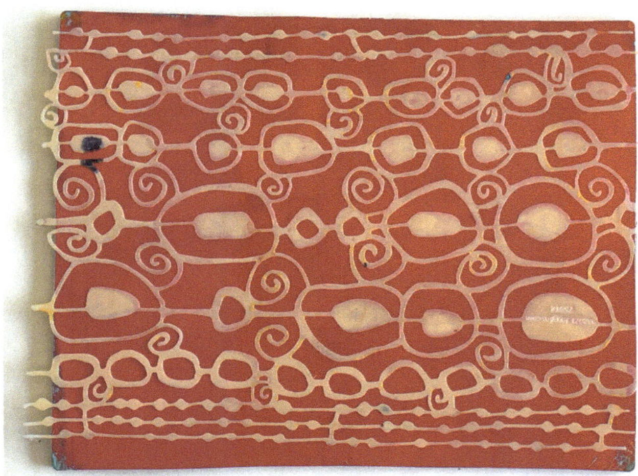

Lay the stencil over a thin layer of paint on the plate in a color (Cadmium Red) that is slightly darker than your base layer (Pyrolle Orange).

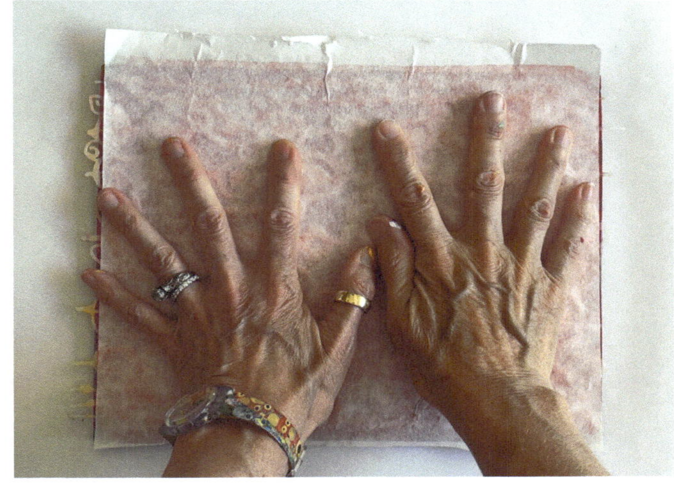

Apply pressure with the heels of the palms of your hands and your fingertips to get good contact with the paper.

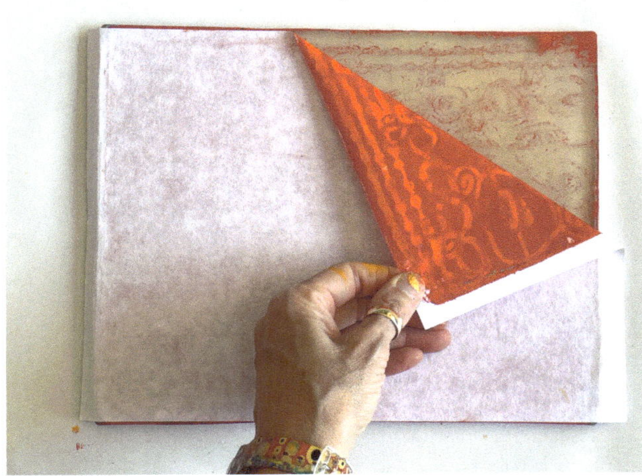

Pull up one corner to peek at your results before you dismount the paper from the plate. Apply more pressure to the paper for a more complete print if needed.

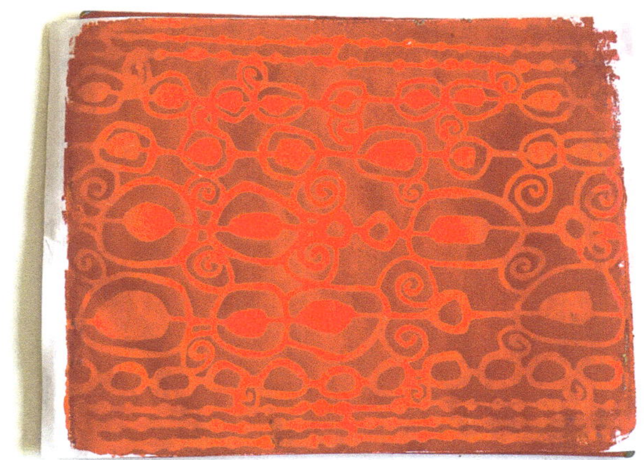

Pull the print.

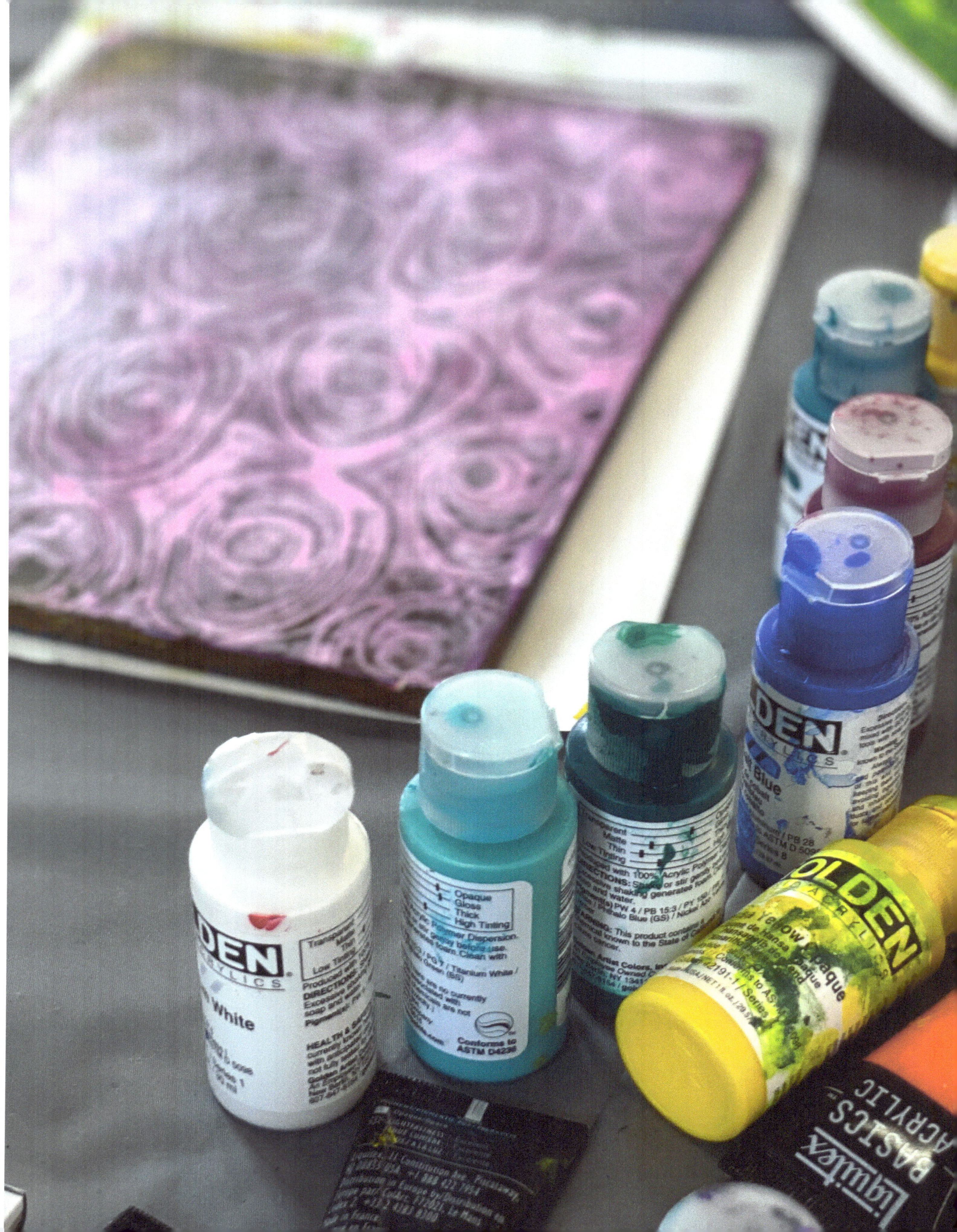

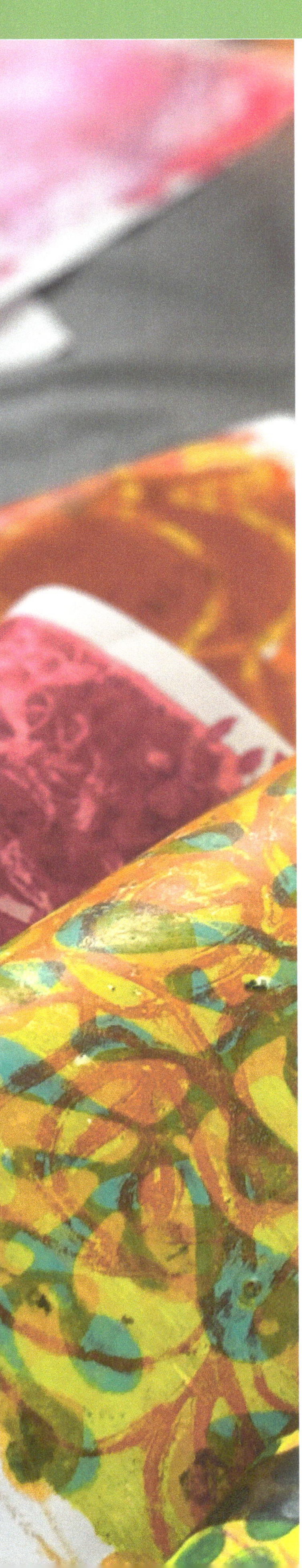

CHAPTER

3 Layering Prints

Once you have the hang of basic prints you are ready to start layering! Mixing and matching several different techniques with stencils and masks over one another creates a rich, layered look with texture and depth. You may practice with just one stencil, but soon you will find yourself wanting more patterns to add to the mix!

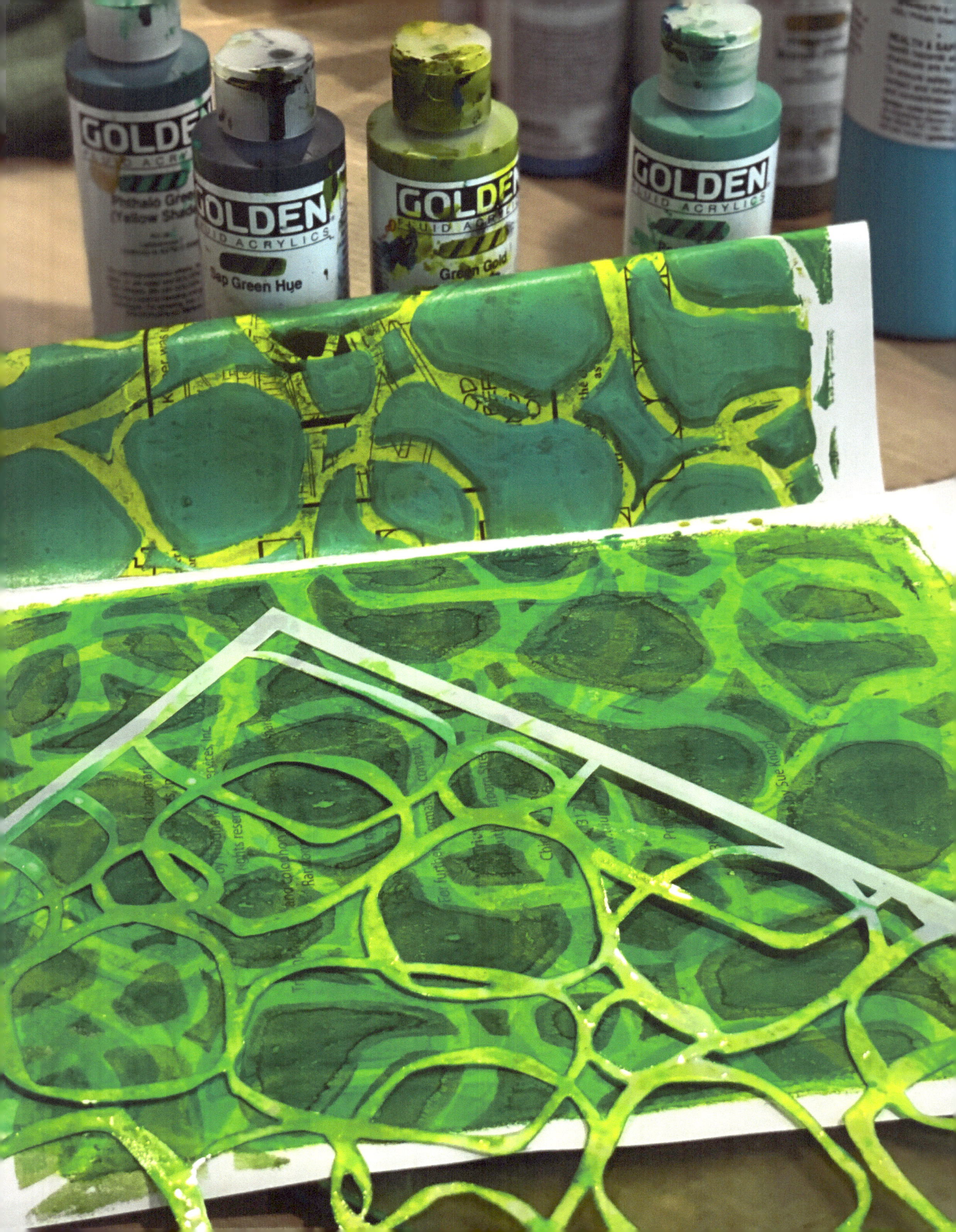
GOLDEN
Phthalo Green
(Yellow Shade)
GOLDEN
Sap Green Hue
GOLDEN
Green Gold
GOLDEN

Building Layers

With Translucent Pigments

Once you have created several light colored base layers your next step is to multiply prints over and over each other in various different ways that will be explained in the following chapters. Because fluid acrylics are varying degrees of translucency, each layer will show through and multiply with the previous print unless that pigment is opaque. Opaque colors should be incorporated as base layers or used sparingly in subsequent layers.

My typical rule of thumb is to combine a minimum of three layers in my gel prints, this creates rich papers for collage with lots and lots of depth. Varying color combinations, stencil and mask patterns, first prints and ghost prints, opaque and transparent colors will create amazing and unique results every time.

Typically, I design my stencil and mask collections to include patterns that layer well with others. I find that combining linear patterns with the curvilinear makes for some unique combinations. I also experiment with layering the ghost print over the first pull print, flipping the direction of the prints so that they don't line up.

Working from light to dark, I try to make subtle shifts in value so that I can achieve multiple layers before I get to dark. You want to go darker slowly... A big jump from light to dark doesn't leave you room for many more layers.

If my goal is to achieve green paper for collage, I'll stay with analogous colors generally, but every rule of thumb is meant to be broken! Experiment with combining complementary colors across the wheel as well.

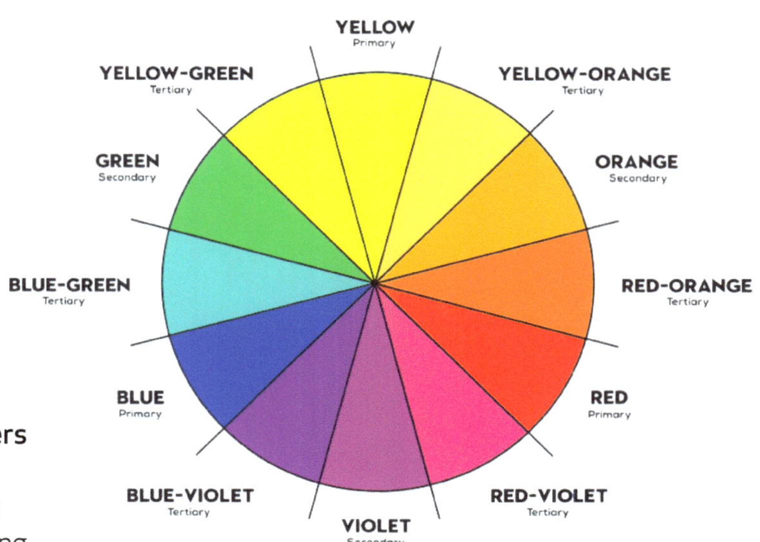

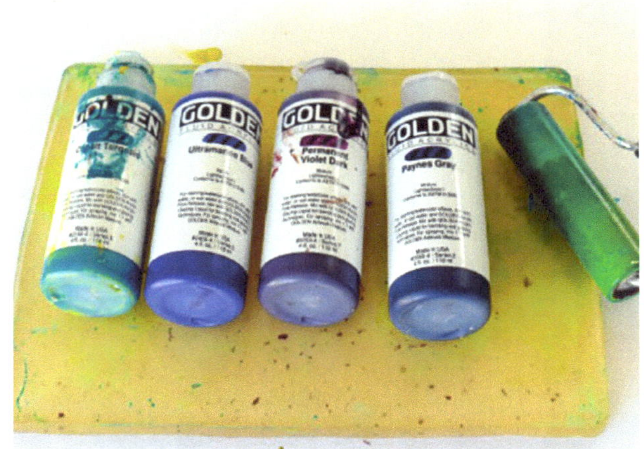

Making use of analogous colors

LAYERING WITH ONE STENCIL

Sometimes keeping it simple to start is a good plan. You can create multi layered prints using just one stencil or mask over and over itself again. When I am working with one stencil or mask, I print the ghost prints over the first print in order to create complex layering. Be sure to keep turning the paper (or the stencil) in a different direction so that the patterns do not line up in your prints.

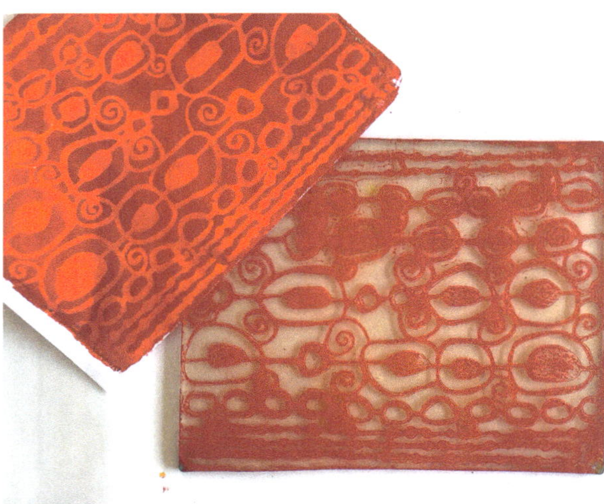

Print your stencil (Cadmium Red) onto your prepared light colored solid (Pyrolle Orange).

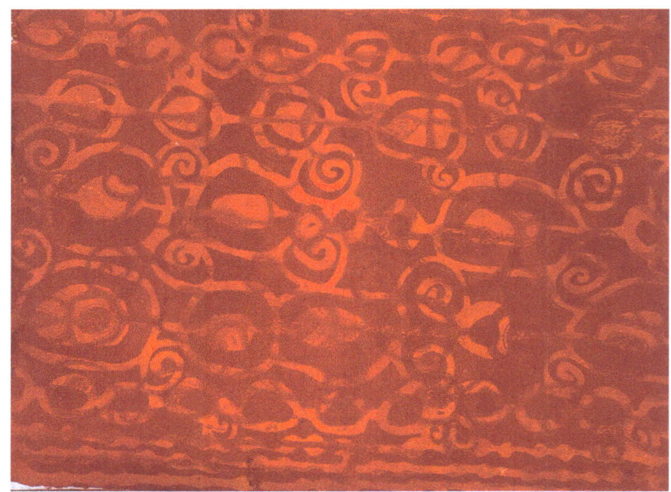

Flip the paper and print the ghost print or leftover paint trapped below the mask, over the first print.

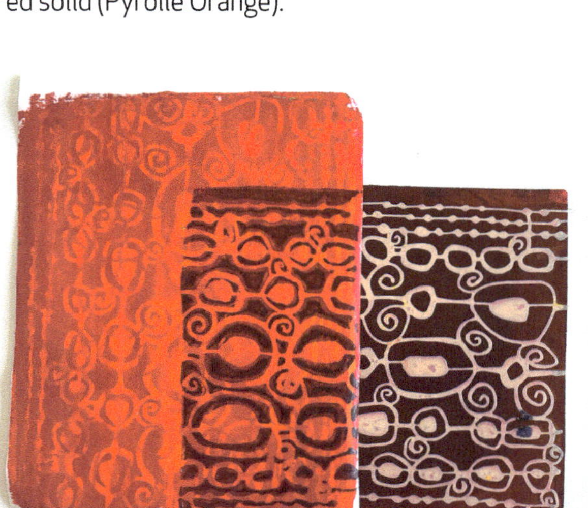

Go a shade darker (Van Dyke Brown) and print again in the opposite direction.

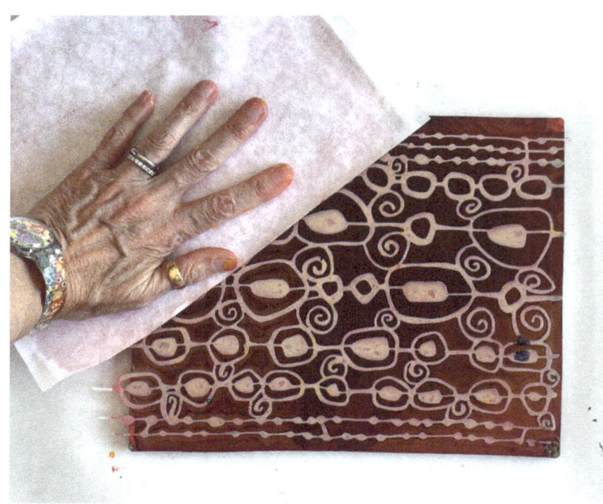

Move your paper around the plate and print overlapping sections of the stencil rather than one straight print, this will help you achieve more complex patterns.

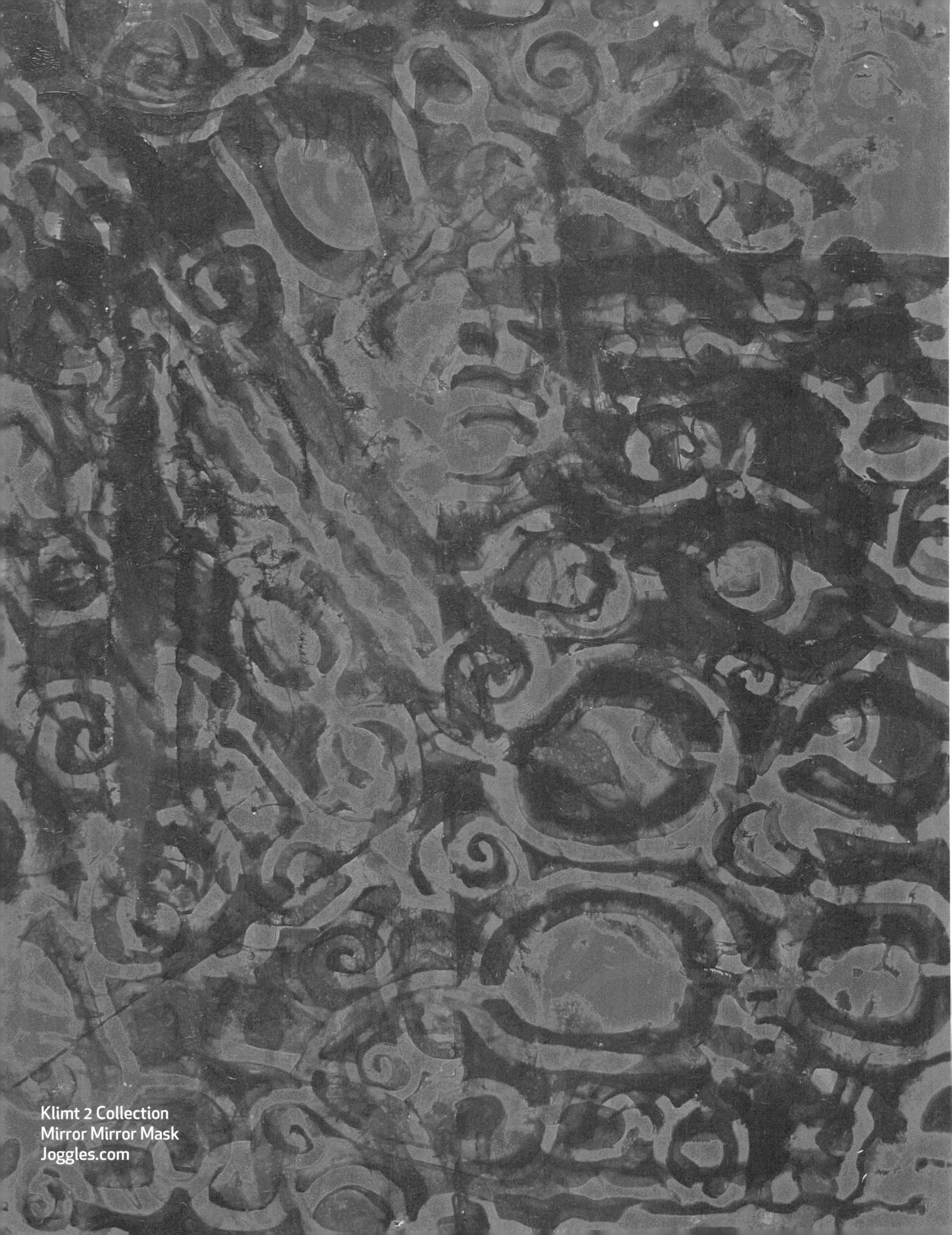
Klimt 2 Collection
Mirror Mirror Mask
Joggles.com

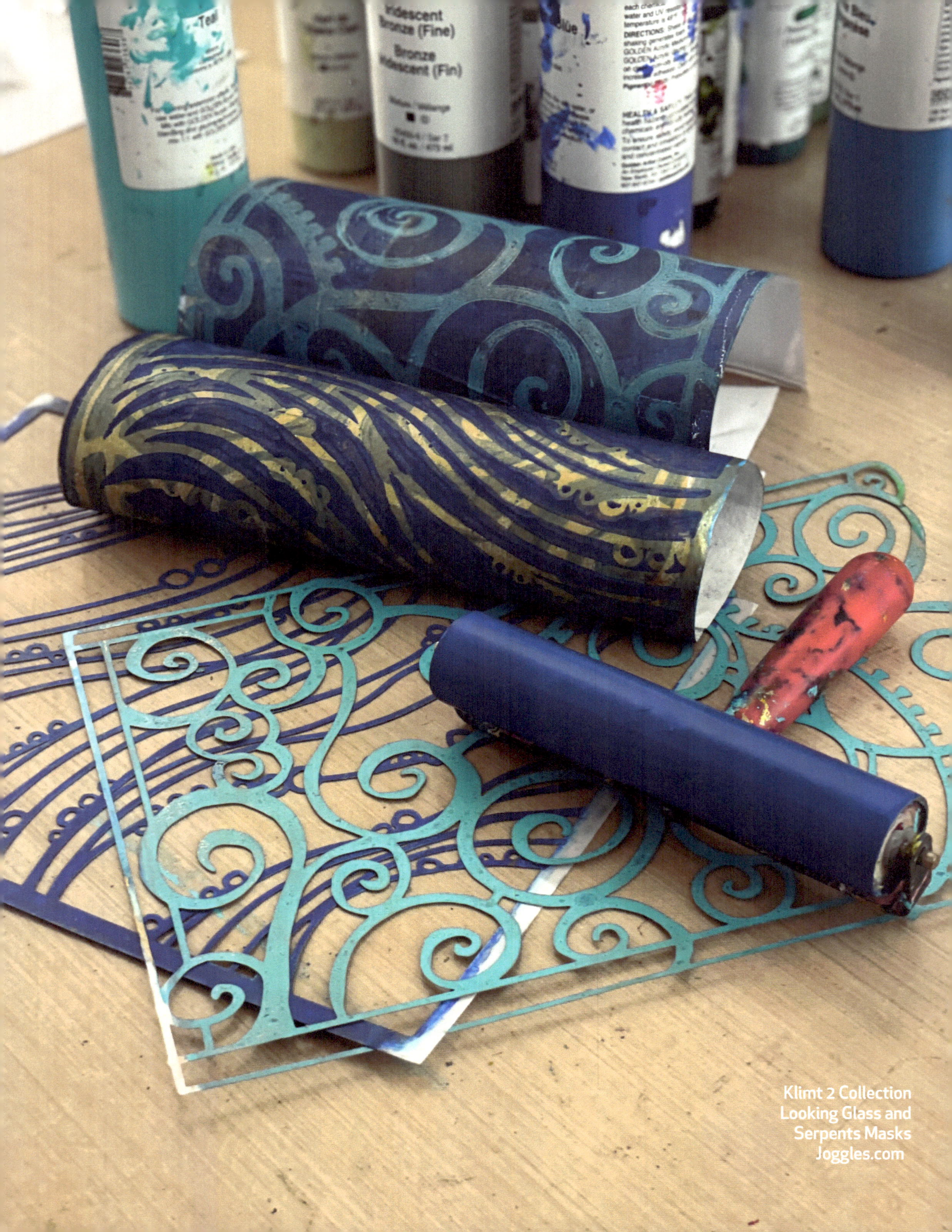
Klimt 2 Collection
Looking Glass and
Serpents Masks
Joggles.com

LAYERING WITH SPECIFIC COMBINATIONS

My stencil and mask designs often include combinations for layering organic with geometric, but there are several good layering options. Look at your stencils and see which two you think would combine well on a print. *Left: Serpents mask layered with Looking Glass. Below: Klimt Collection Rectangle Motif stencil layered with Peacock Collection Ruffled Feathers mask.*

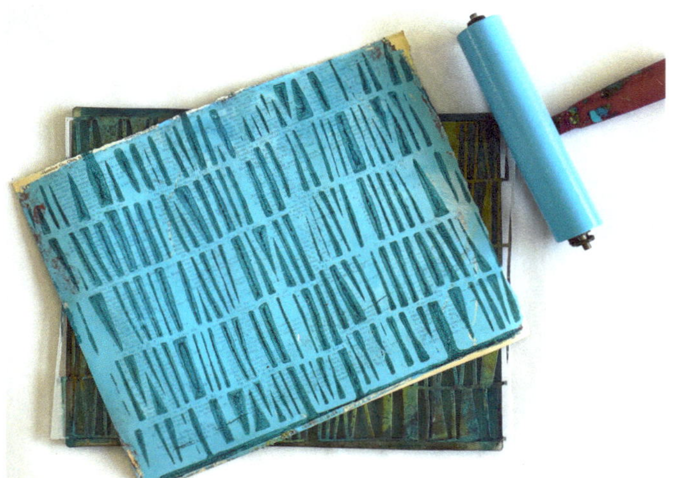

Print your stencil (Turquoise Phthalo) onto your prepared light colored (Teal) solid.

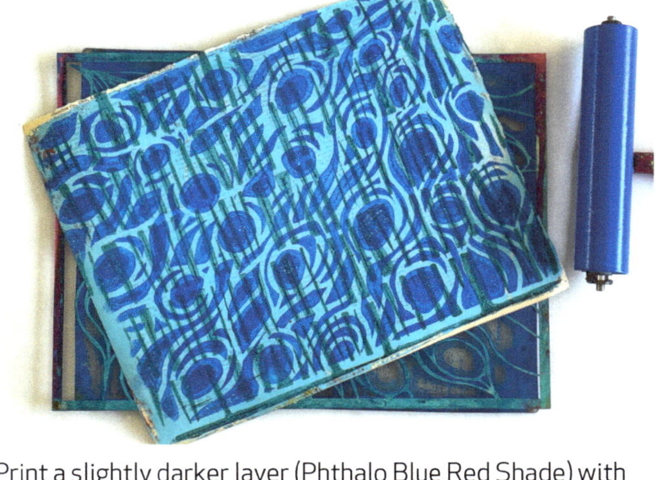

Print a slightly darker layer (Phthalo Blue Red Shade) with your second stencil.

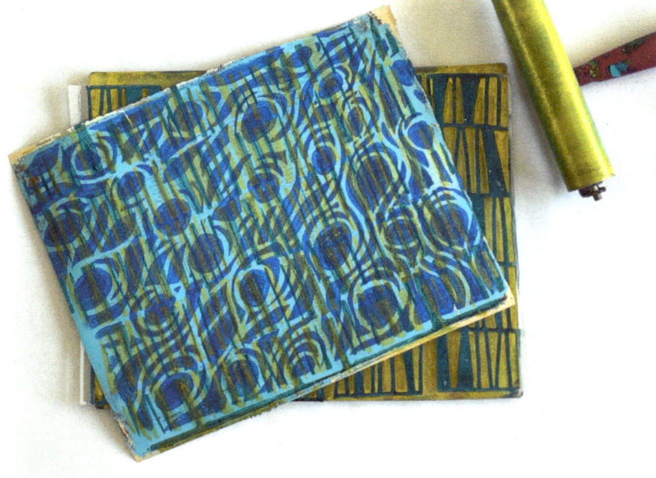

Bring the first stencil back on top for a third layer (Bright Gold Fine) using either darker, metallic, or opaque paint.

TIP: Press off all the remaining wet paint from your stencils and masks onto a clean up sheet of clean, dry paper. This is the best way to keep your supplies clean. Acrylic paint, once dry, is not going to wash off. You may also consider keeping a dish basin of warm soapy water to toss them (and your brayers) into while the paint is still wet.

Building Layers

With Opaque Pigments

You can take a print or prints that you feel are too busy and give them new life with opaque layers on top. When you use gesso, metallics, or other opaque pigments in combination with a mask, the process allows only the area of the original print that is under the mask to show through. This makes your busy or unsuccessful gel print act simply as a color field for the pattern of the mask.

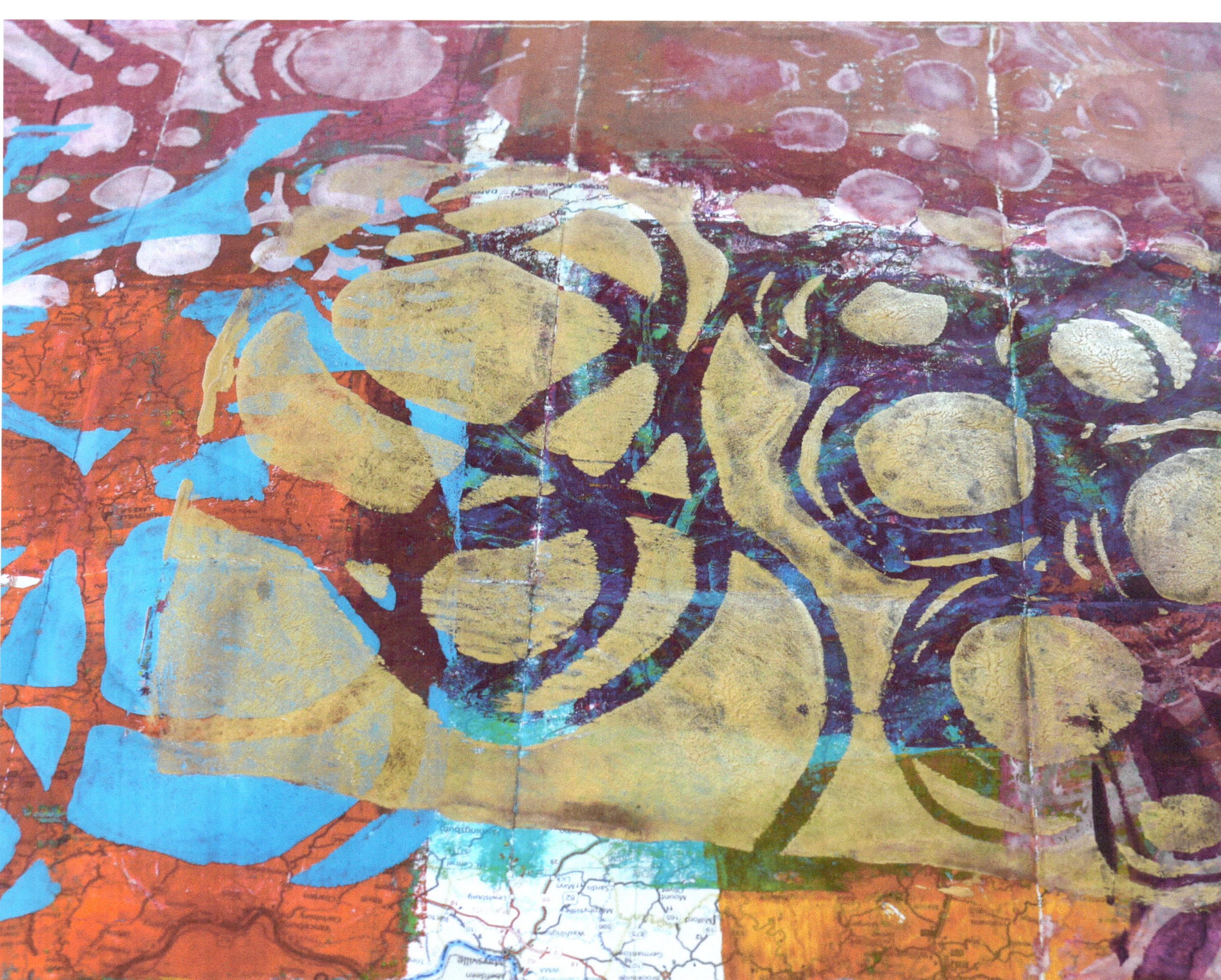

OPAQUE LAYERS ON TOP

When looking for opaque colors, refer to the swatch of paint on the front of your Golden Fluid Acrylics container to determine the level of opacity of your colors. All metallics are considered opaque, plus a handful of additional colors. You may also use white gesso alone or blended with other colors to create an opaque layer. NOTE: adding white gesso will make your colors lighter, more pastel in tone.

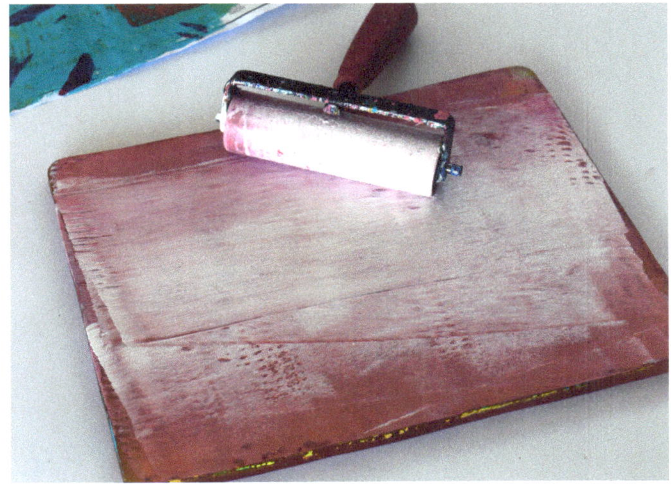

Roll out a thin layer of white gesso onto the plate with or without added pigment.

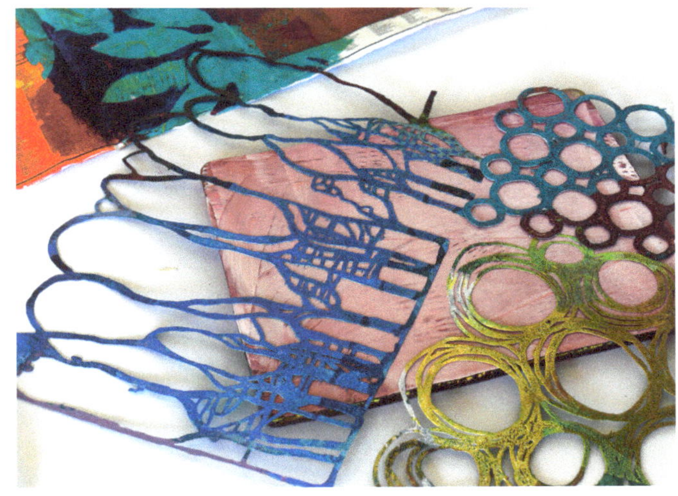

Lay stencils into the gesso.

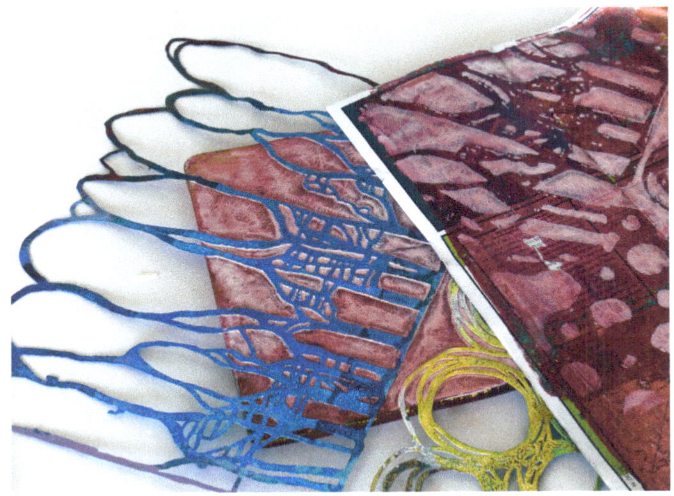

Use a previous print as your base layer.

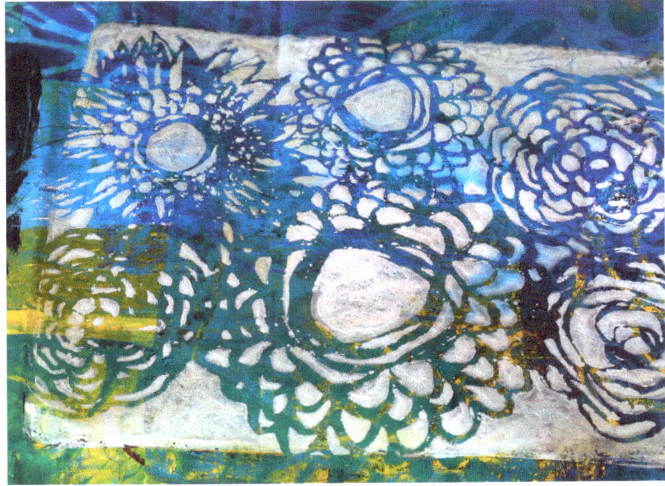

Gesso or opaque paint will not allow anything to show through but the pattern from the mask.

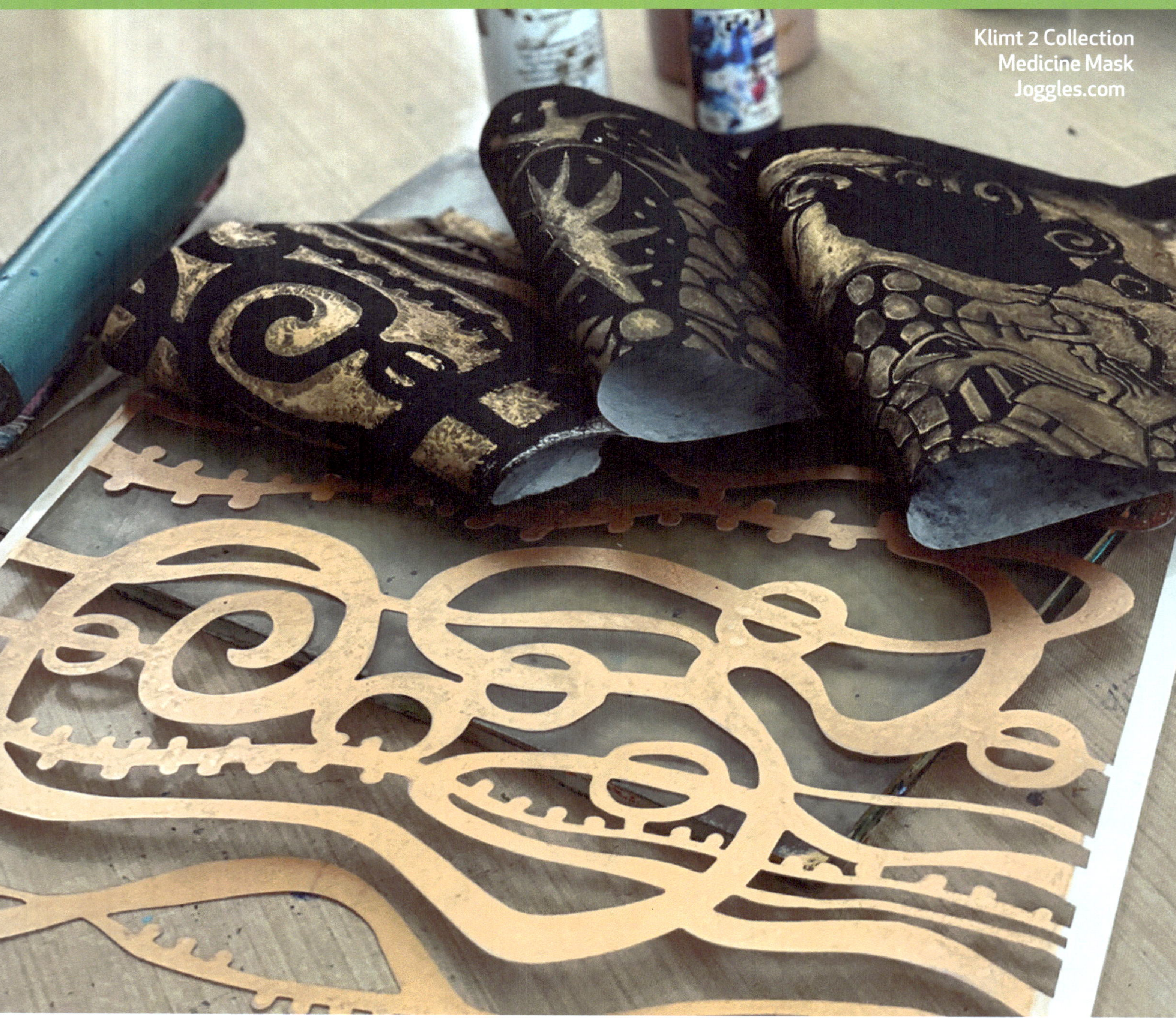

METALLIC

Opaque paints cover darks like black or deep purple beautifully. One of the most dramatic pairings I have found is metallic with black. The prints above were created with 9x12 Joggles masks from the Gustav Klimt Inspired 2 series. In keeping with the Gustav Klimt theme, I painted rice paper with black gesso and then gel printed with Golden Fluid Acrylic Copper (opaque) on top. Another favorite opaque color to try over black is Teal.

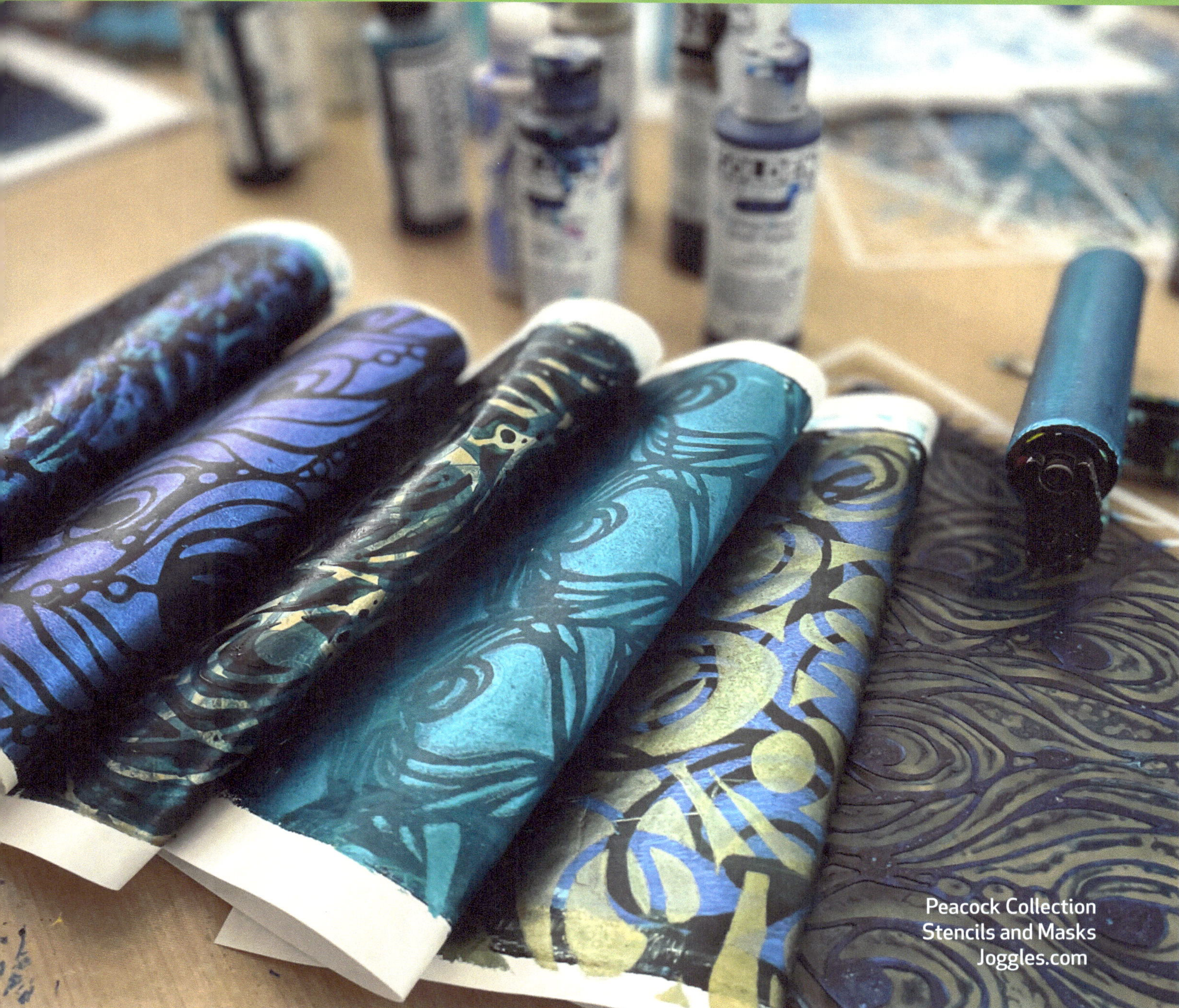

INTERFERENCE AND IRIDESCENT

In addition to metallics, Golden's Interference and Iridescent colors also look amazing over dark colors. These colors give a taffeta fabric effect in that they are most dramatic when angled toward the light. In the above sheets I have printed Interference Blue over Paynes gray (second from left) and Interference Green/Blue over Phthalo Turquoise (fourth from left). Layering being key, you can also layer metallics over the interference like Bronze over Interference Blue over Paynes Gray (fifth from left). Remember that you can blend interference and metallic in with other Fluid Acrylic colors to create interesting new colors that will also stand up over dark.

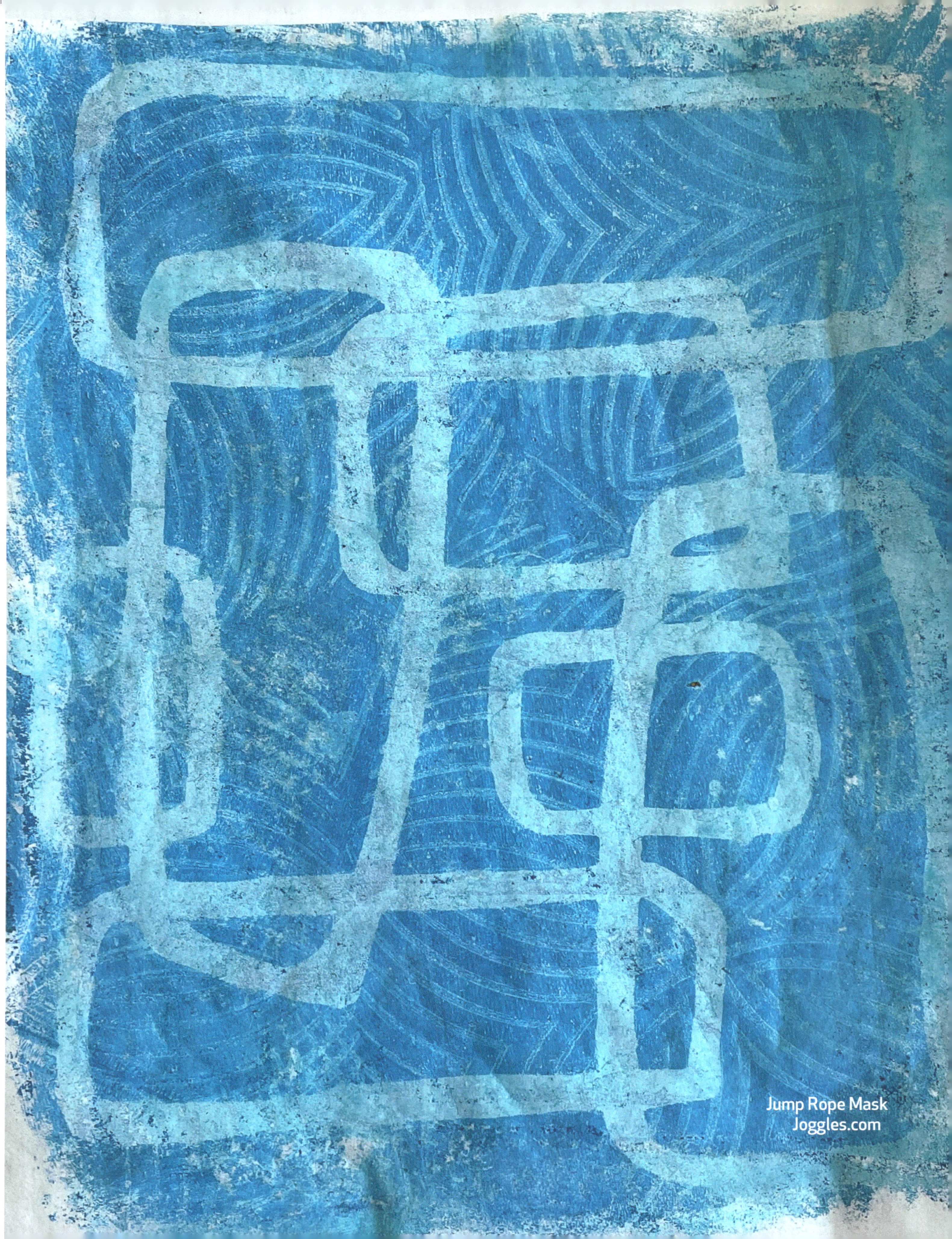
Jump Rope Mask
Joggles.com

ADDING TEXTURE TO LAYERS

Pressing and removing a textured object into the paint layer will create a subtle pattern in the paint before you add your stencil/mask. I have texture rubbing plates that I use often for this effect, they come in a set of may different patterns and have emboss on one side and deboss on the other, each gives a slightly different effect.

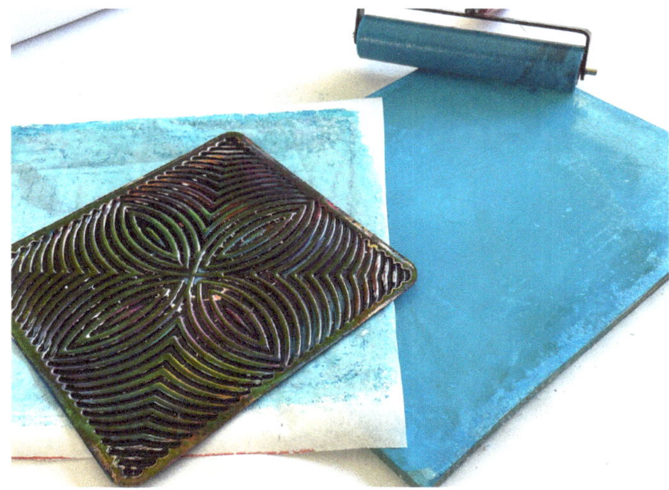

Roll out a thin layer of (Manganese Blue) paint on the plate that is slightly darker than your light colored solid (Teal).

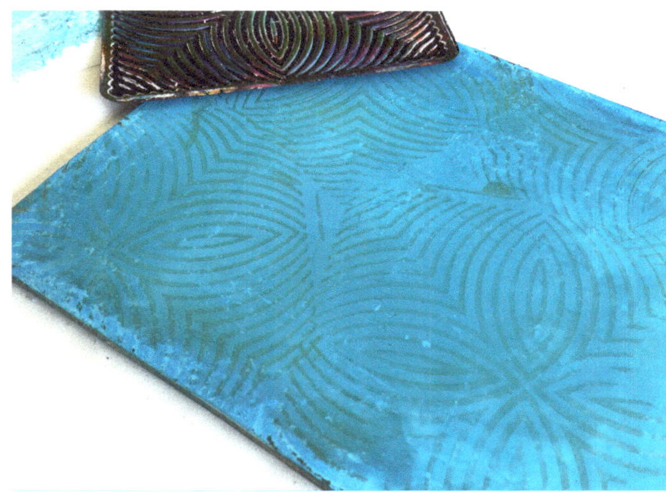

Press a texture plate into the paint to create a pattern before applying the stencil or mask.

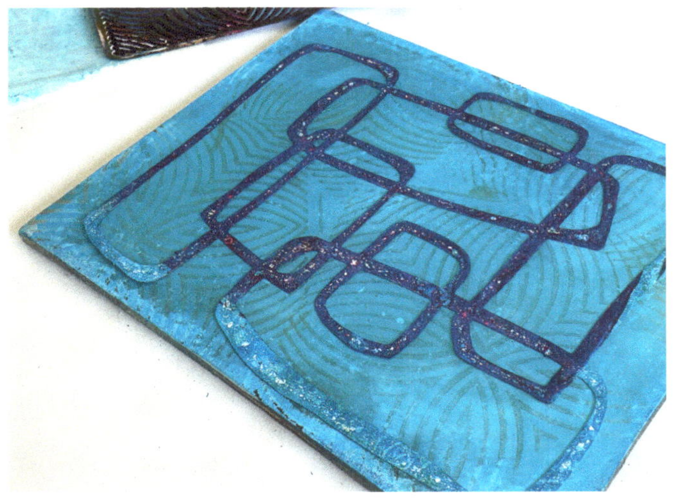

Put your mask into the paint.

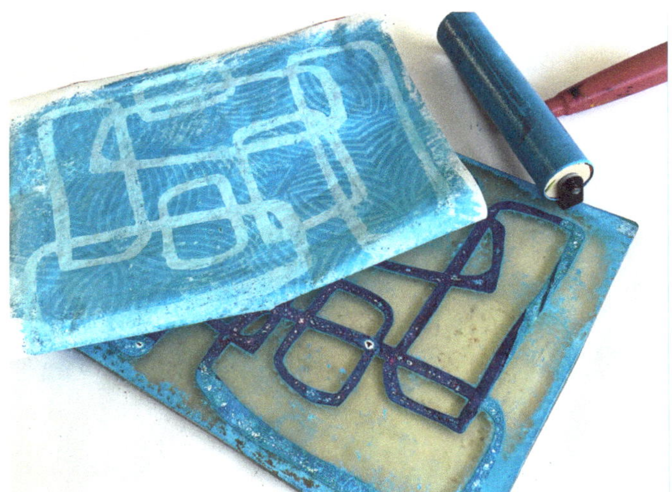

Print the layer.

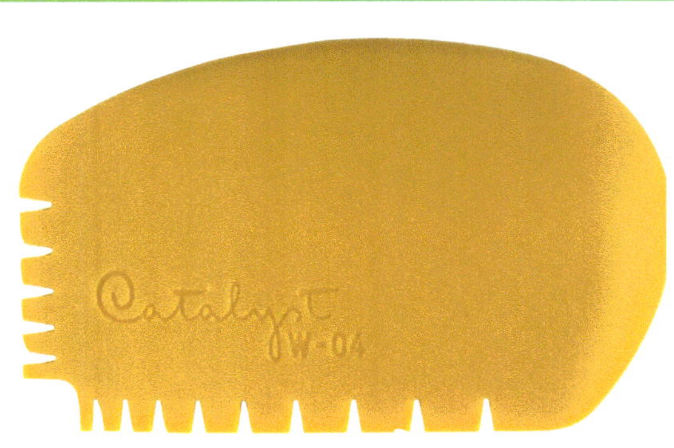

ADDING TEXTURE TO LAYERS

Princeton makes a line of hand held wedge tools with teeth on two edges. They fit nicely in the palm of your hand and come in many different widths and patterns for scraping. The wedges work wonderfully on the gel printing plate to scrape straight, wiggled, zig-zag, or any combination of motions to create interesting patterns.

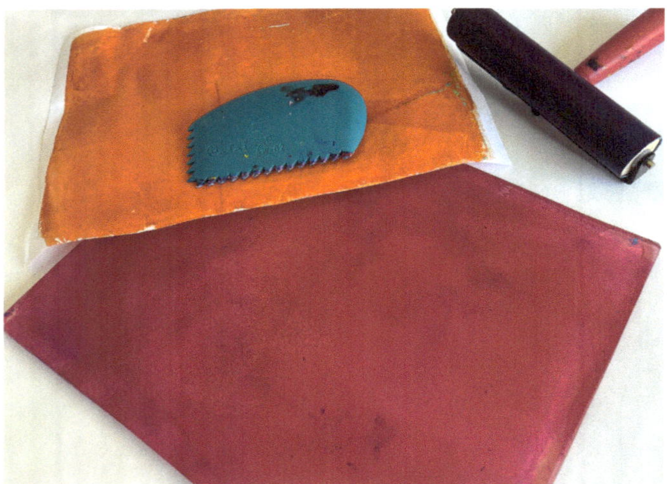

Roll out a thin layer of paint (Quinacridone Magenta) on the plate that is slightly darker than your previous layer (Pyrolle Orange).

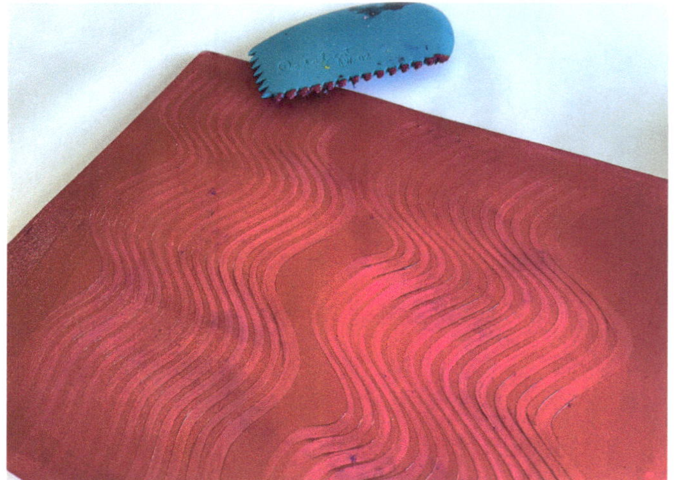

Remove paint from the plate with the scrapers before applying the stencil or mask.

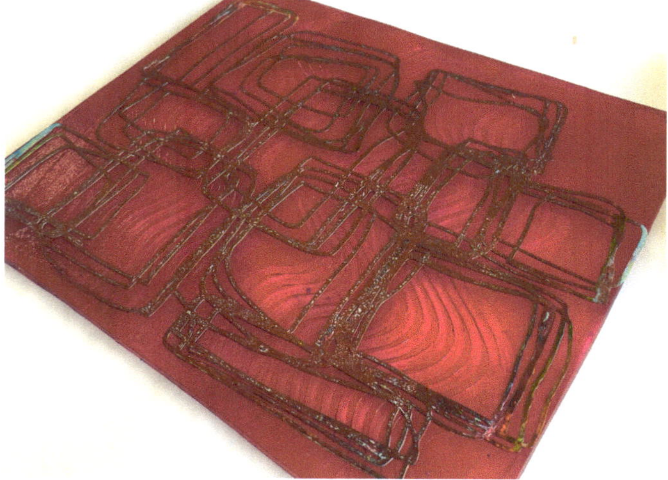

Put the stencil or mask into the textured layer.

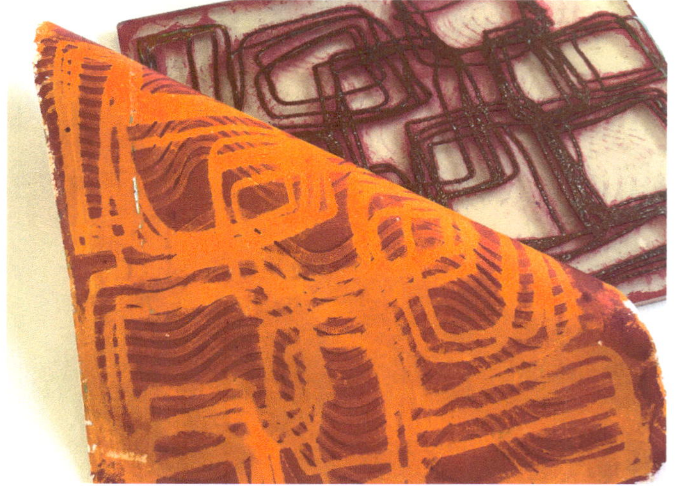

Print the layer .

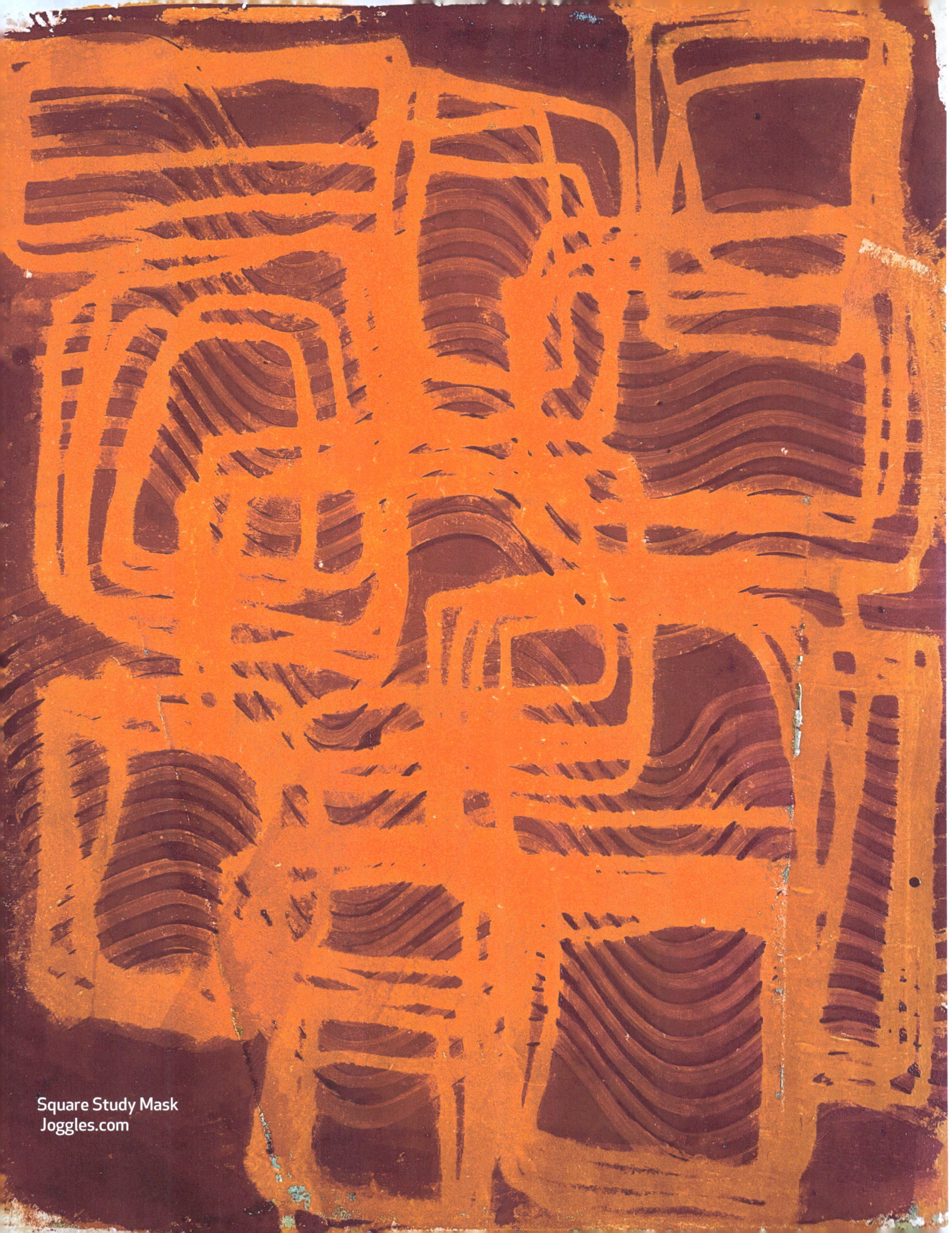
Square Study Mask
Joggles.com

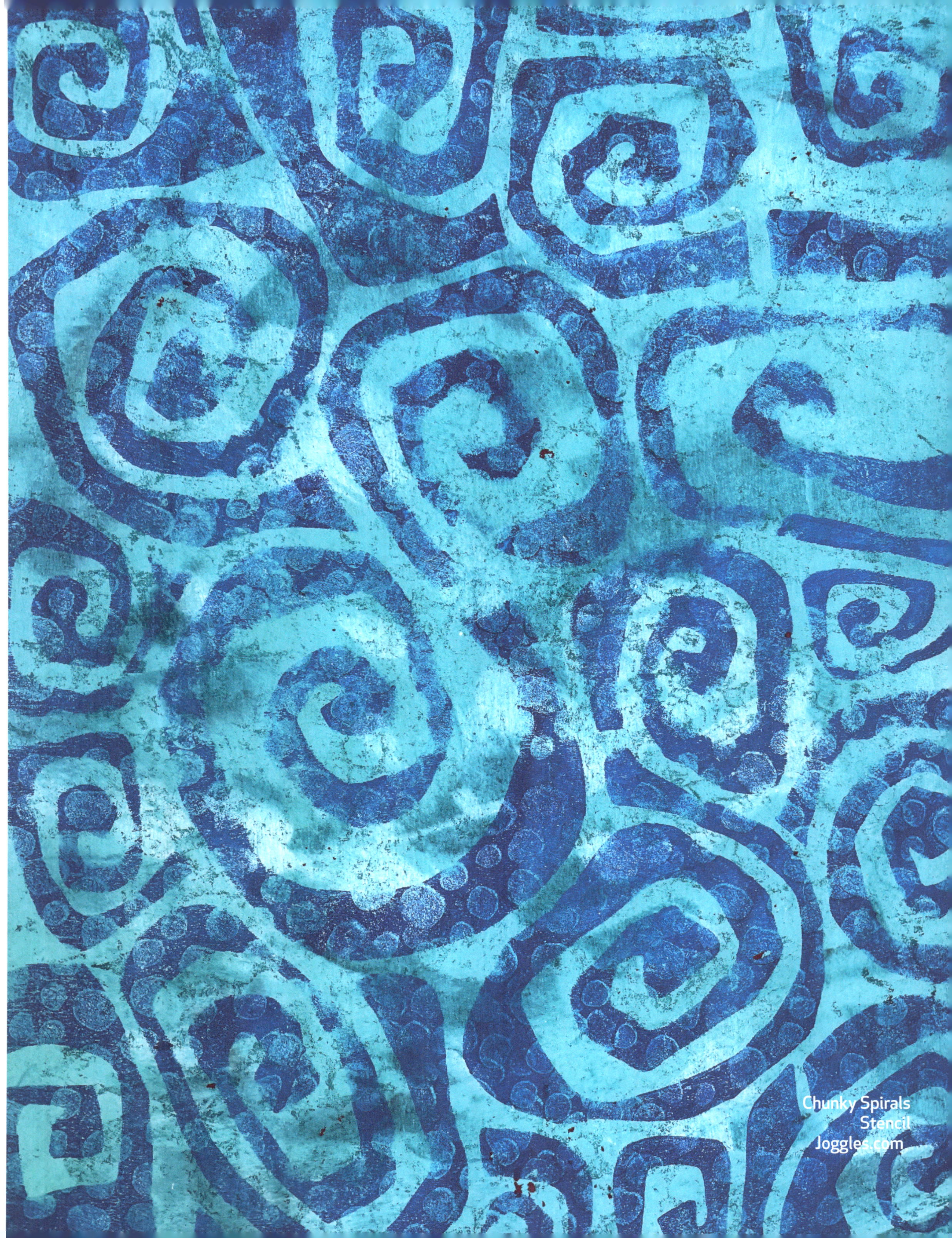
Chunky Spirals
Stencil
Joggles.com

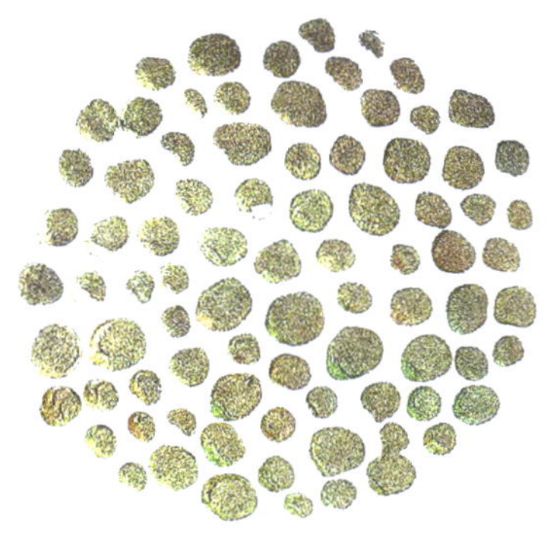

ADDING TEXTURE TO LAYERS

Foam or rubber stamps can be pressed into paint on the plate before applying the stencil or mask to add texture. Be sure to overlap and intersect your stamps to create a complex pattern, resist the temptation to stamp them out separately like cookies on a baking sheet! *Below: Seed Pod foam stamp, my design for Joggles.*

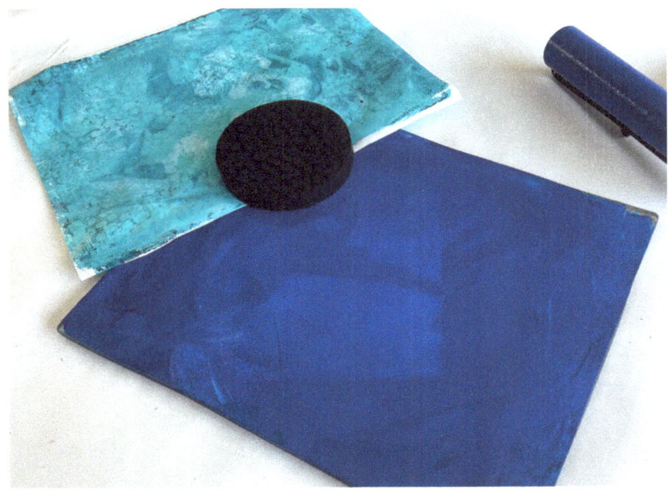

Roll out a thin layer of paint (Phthalo Blue Red Shade) on the plate that is slightly darker than your light colored solid (Teal blended with Titanium White).

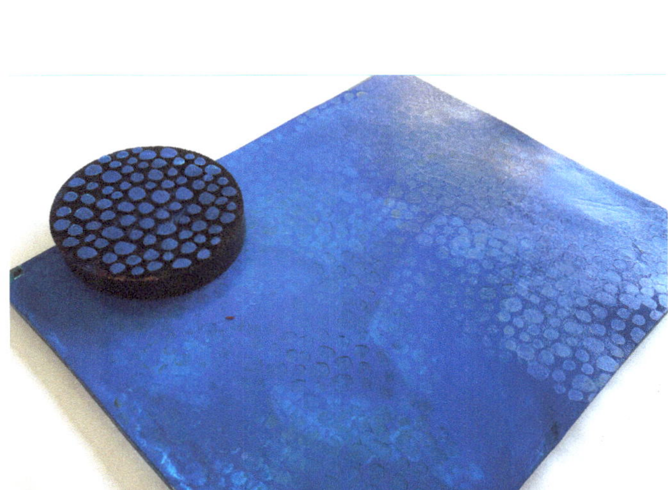

Stamp into the paint to make a pattern before applying the stencil or mask.

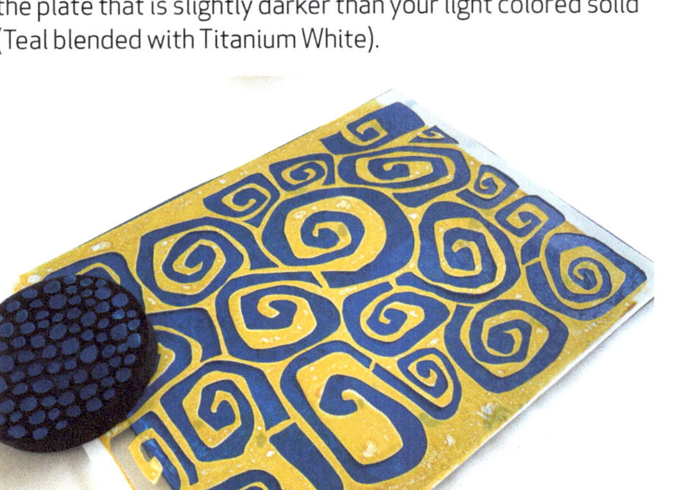

Put your stencil into the paint.

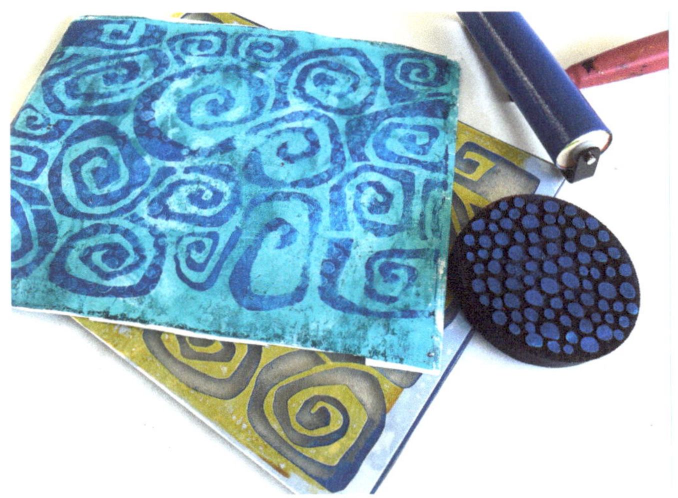

Print the layer.

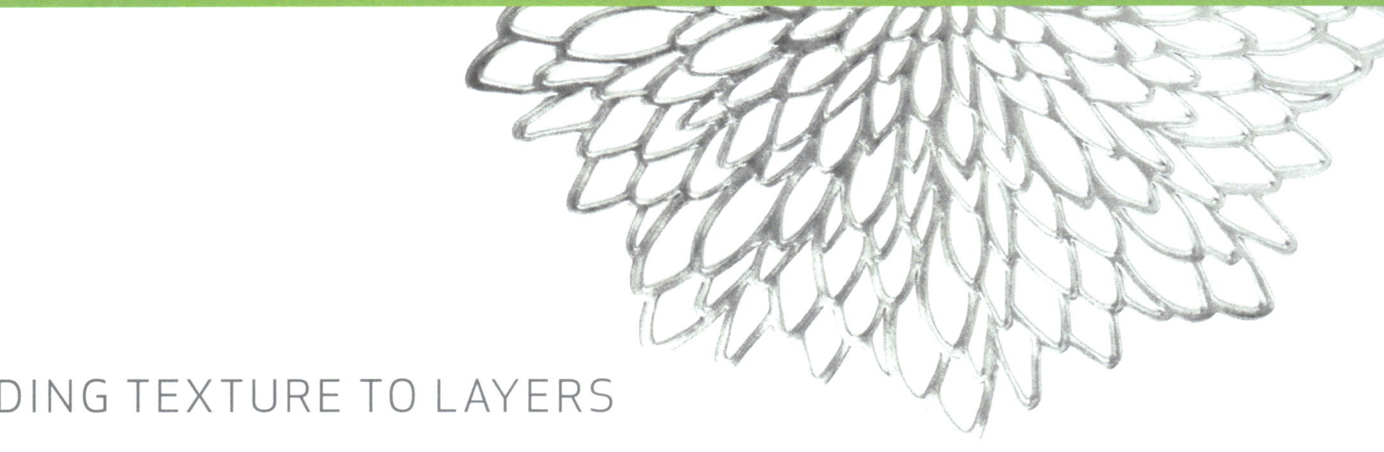

ADDING TEXTURE TO LAYERS

Look for household items that might impress a pattern into the paint on the gel plate before adding a stencil. One of my favorite texture tools is a silicone sink liner or place mat, you can often get these at the dollar store.

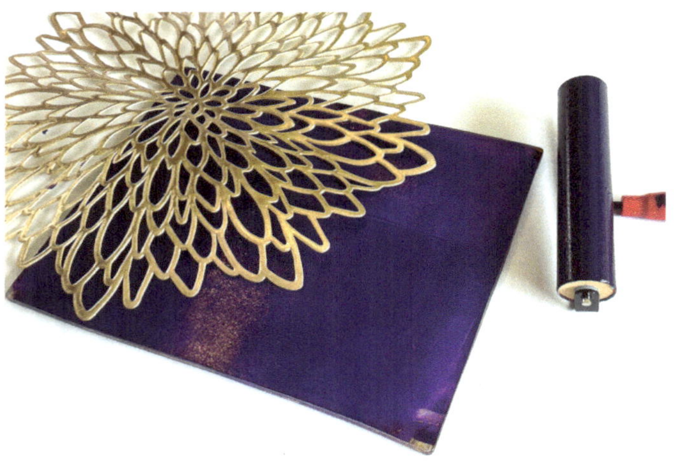

Roll out a thin layer of paint on the plate (Dioxazine Purple) that is slightly darker than your previous layer (DP mixed with Titanium White). Lay the place mat into it.

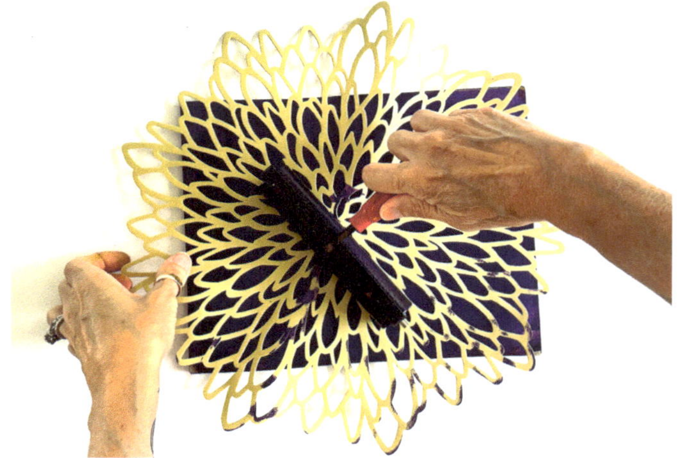

Use the brayer to press the place mat into the paint, keeping your fingertips from touching the surface.

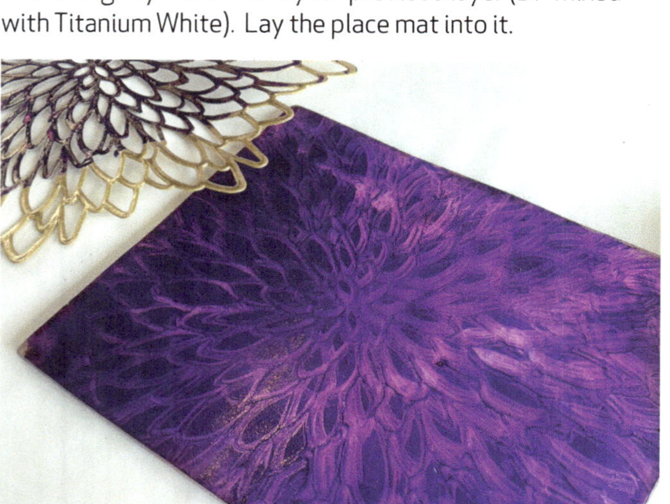

Lift the place mat out of the paint to reveal the pattern.

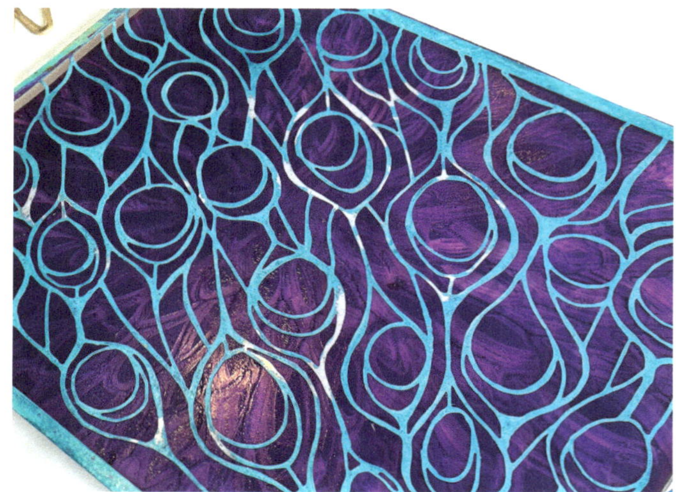

Place a stencil into the paint and print the layer .

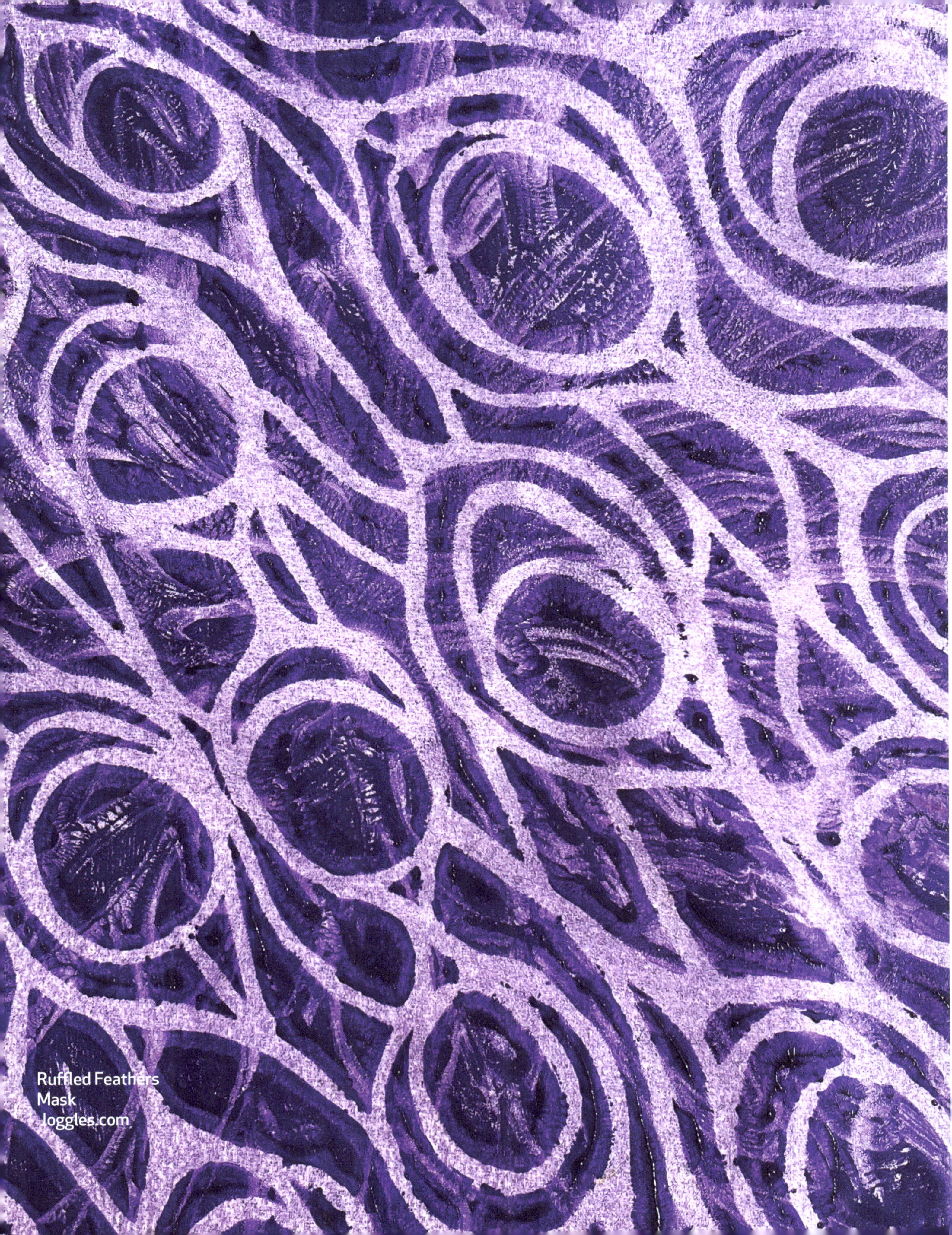
Ruffled Feathers
Mask
loggles.com

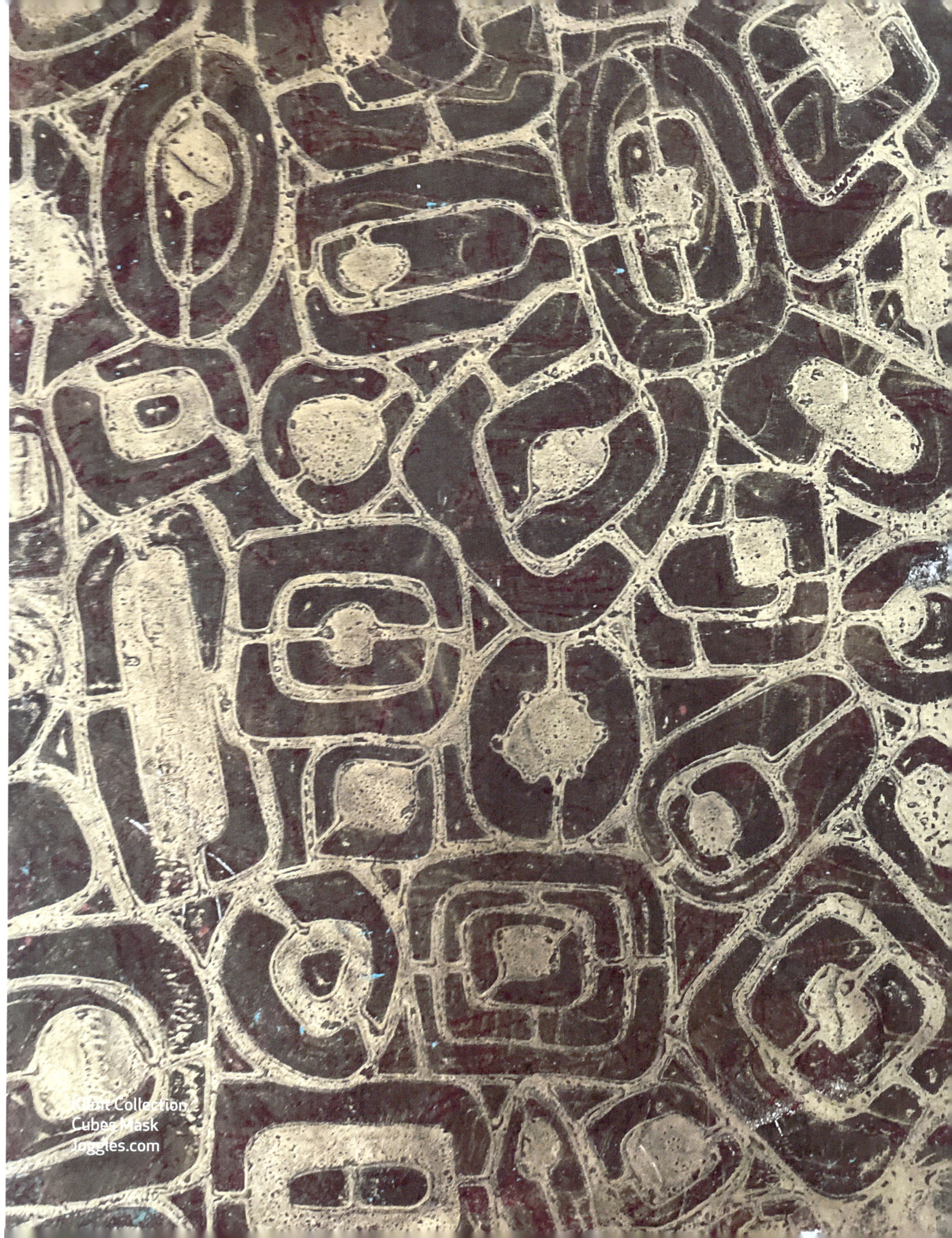

Kfast Collection
Cubes Mask
Joggles.com

CHAPTER

4 Ghost Printing

A ghost print is an impression you get from the paint that has been trapped beneath your stencil or mask after you pull your initial print. Ghost prints can be utilized in several different ways; you can transfer your ghost print to a prepared light colored solid, you can multiply it over the first print, or you can let it dry on the plate and pull it with additional paint onto a new sheet of paper–the combinations are endless.

GHOST PRINT COMPARED TO FIRST PRINT

The ghost print is a softer, more organic print than the first print of a stencil or mask which is typically crisp and more graphic. The soft edges of the ghost print give it a more painterly look, this process of making two prints from each impression offers very different results from the same stencil or mask!

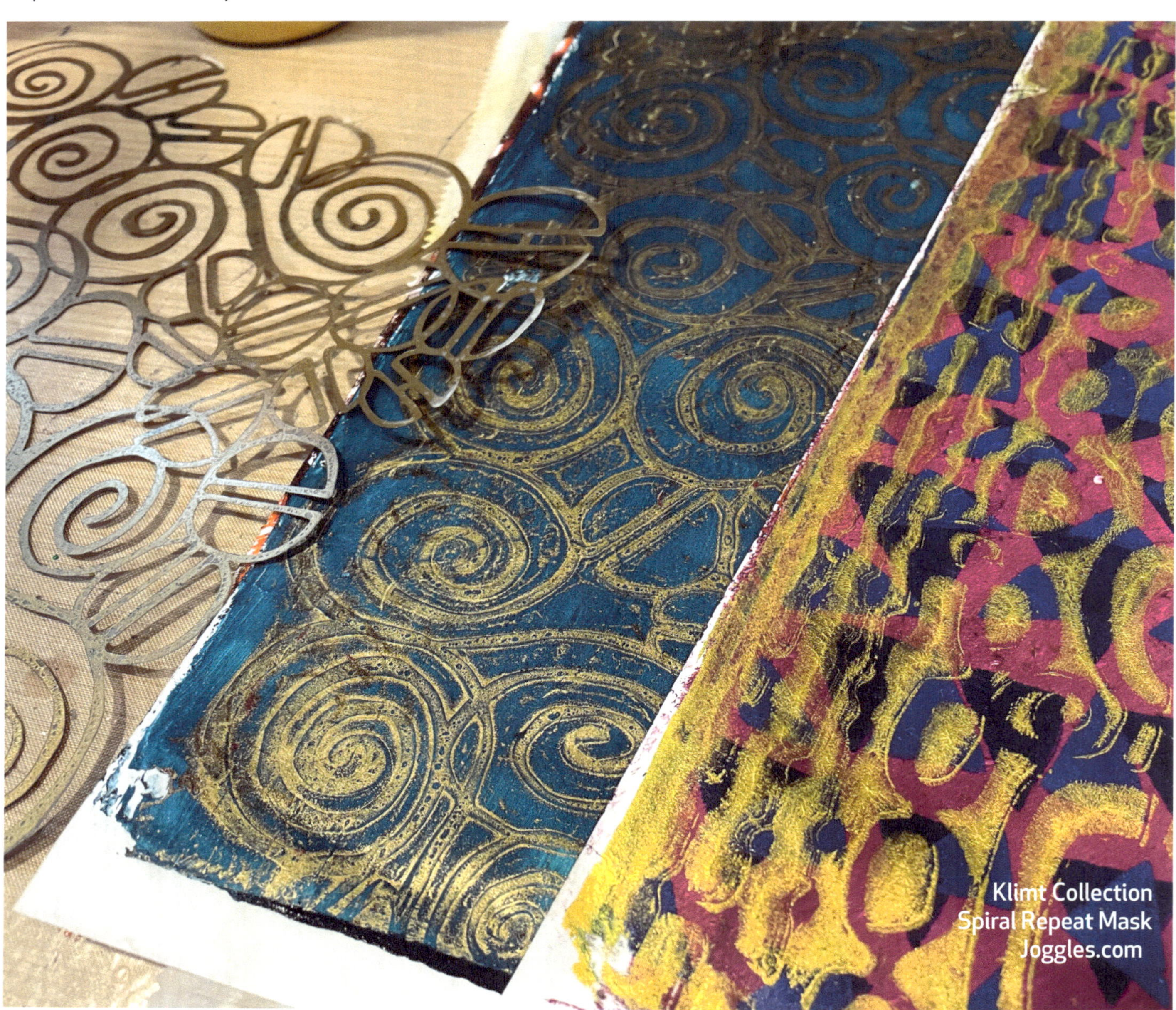

TRANSFERRING GHOST PRINTS TO SOLIDS

One way to use ghost prints is to transfer them immediately onto a prepared light colored solid–have these papers ready and close by as the ghost print needs to be pulled quickly before it dries on the plate. Be sure to have enough contrast between your solid and your ghost print colors.

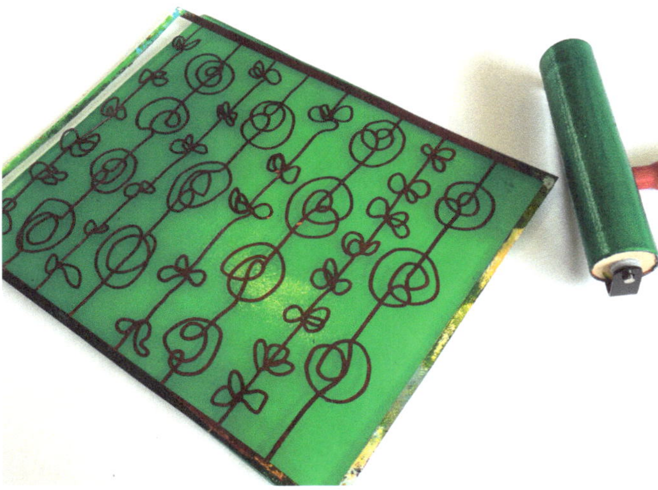

Lay the mask (Poppies) over a thin layer of (Permanent Green Light) paint on the plate that is slightly darker than your base layer.

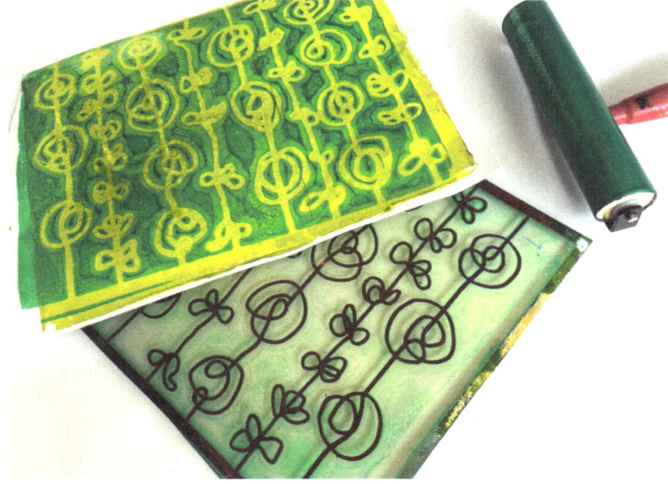

Press and pull a print from the plate, leaving behind the paint that's trapped beneath the mask.

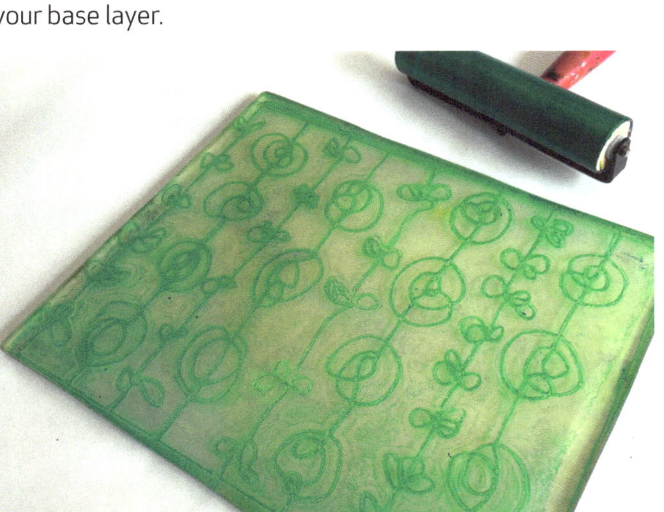

Paint left behind becomes the ghost print, or second print, after removing the mask.

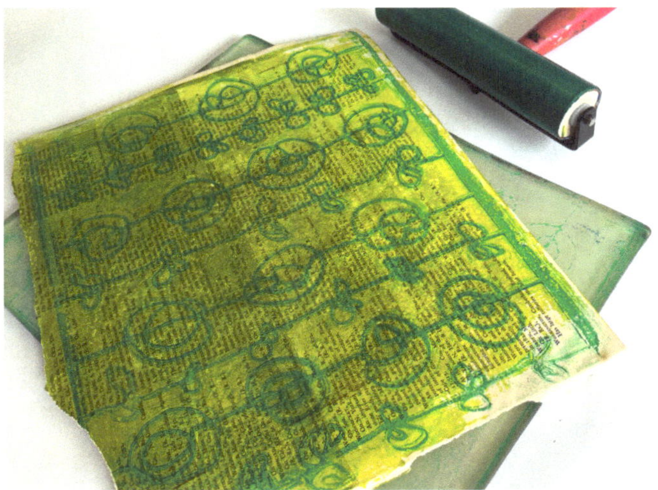

Transfer the ghost print to a prepared light colored solid (Green Gold).

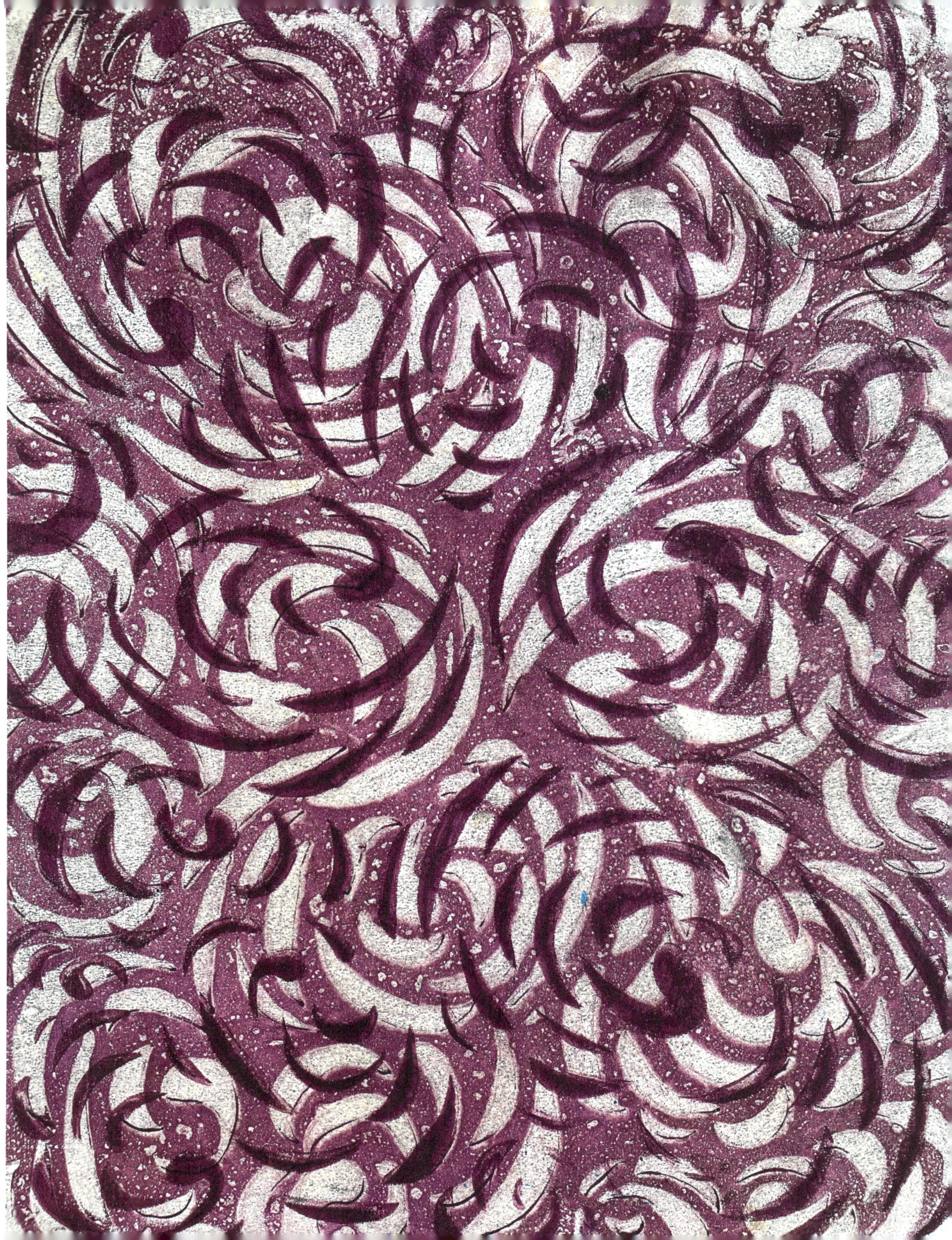

LAYERING FIRST PRINTS WITH GHOST PRINTS

The ghost print can be layered over the first print for harmony of patterns. When I do this I typically flip the first print so that I am layering the ghost print over it in the opposite direction. You may also try layering it in the same direction for two different effects. *Below: Van Gogh Spirals mask design for Joggles.com.*

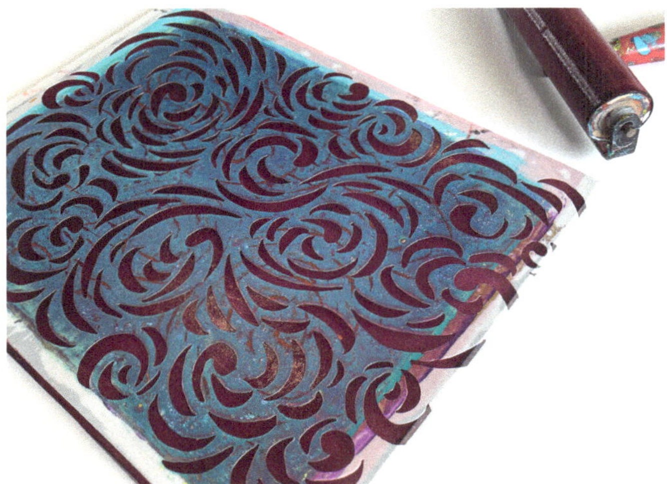

Lay the stencil over a thin layer of paint (Quinacridone Magenta) on the plate.

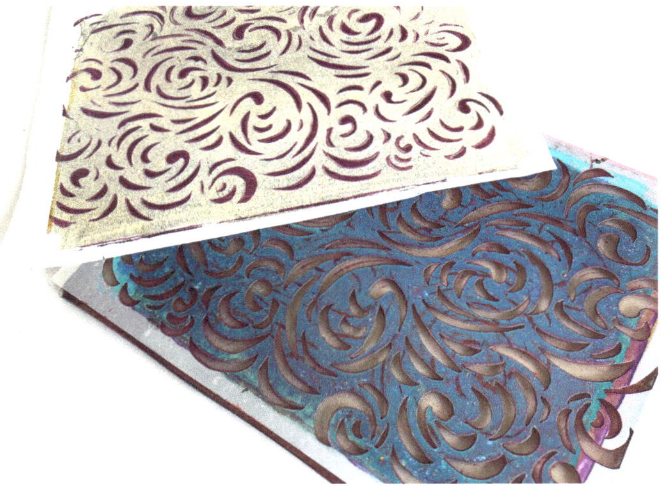

Press and pull a print over your light colored solid (Iridescent Pearl Fine).

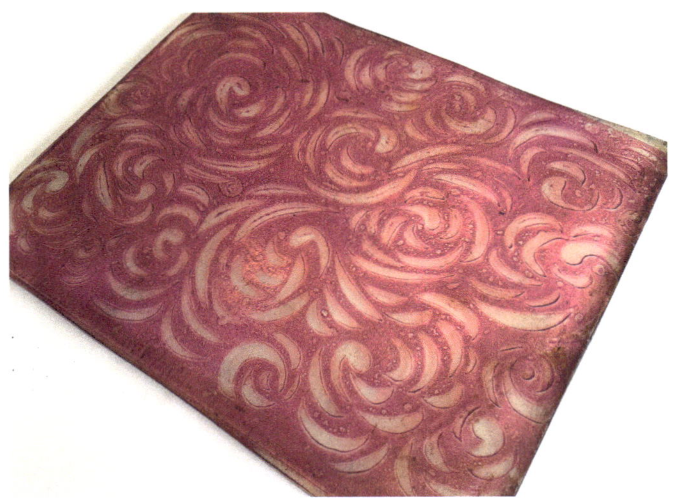

Paint left behind becomes the ghost print, or second print, after removing the stencil.

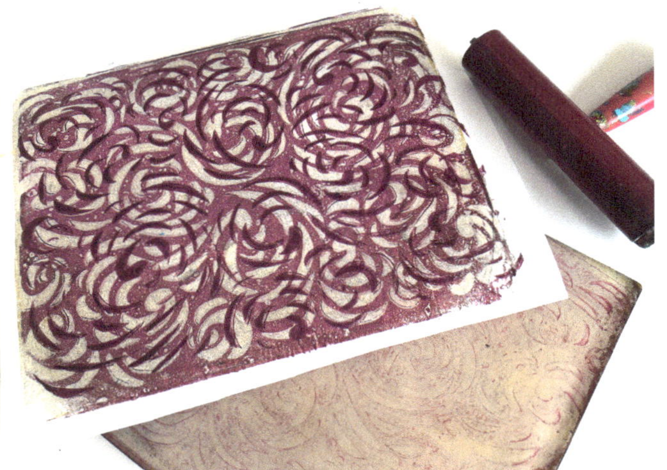

Transfer the ghost print to your first print, flipping the direction of your paper so that the patterns do not line up.

TRANSFERRING GHOST PRINTS WITH PAINT

A second way to use ghost prints is to let the paint dry on the plate and then add another full layer of paint over the top and pull a print with both layers. The moisture of the second layer of paint will cause the plate to release the dry ghost print layer. Be sure to have enough contrast between your second paint color and your ghost print.

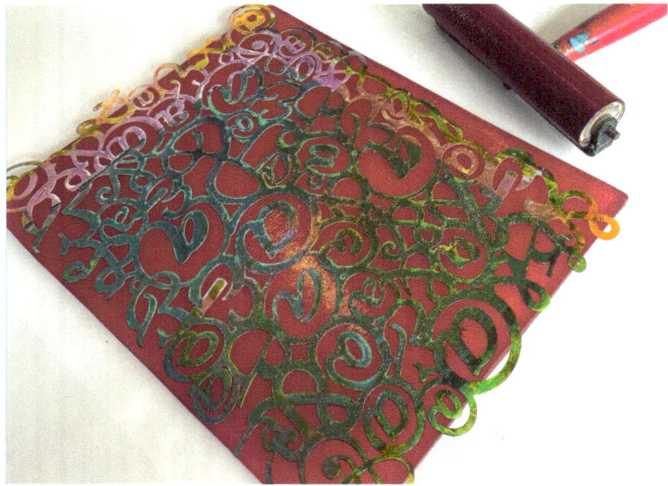

Press and pull a print from the plate on scrap paper (Quinacridone Magenta).

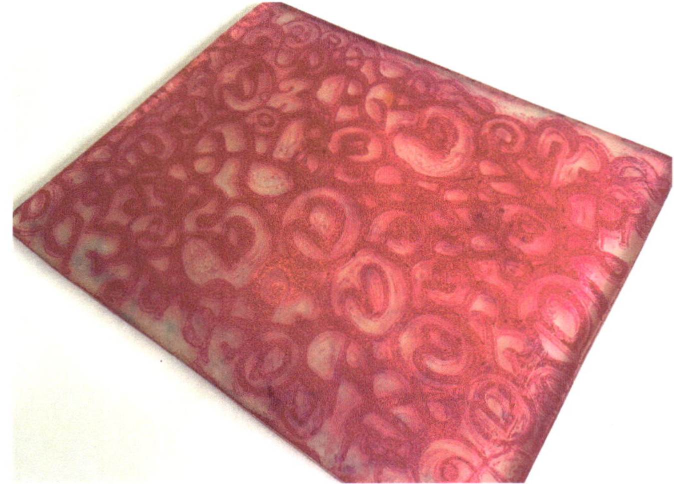

Paint left behind becomes the ghost print, allow this to dry.

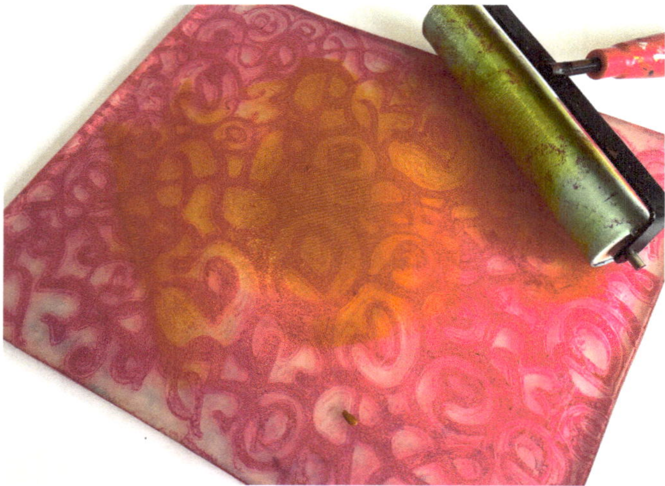

Apply a layer of paint (Indian Yellow) in a contrasting color over the plate.

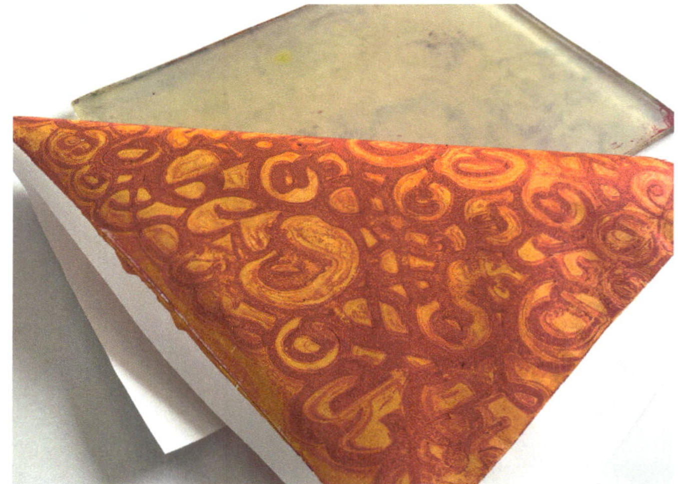

Apply generous pressure and pull the print.

Ultimately this ghost print was embellished with another paint layer plus glitter.
Below: At Ampersand mask design for Joggles.com.

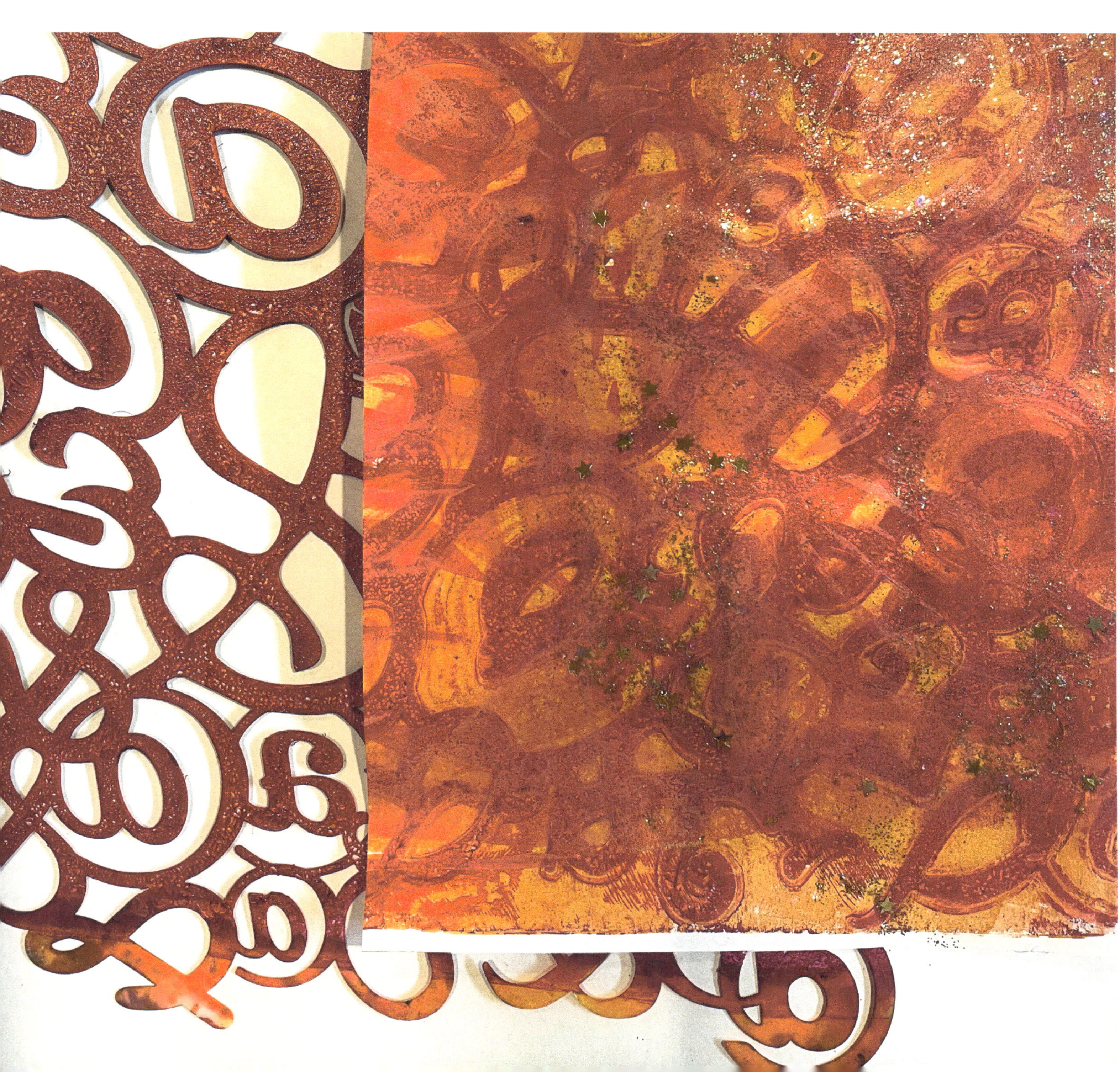

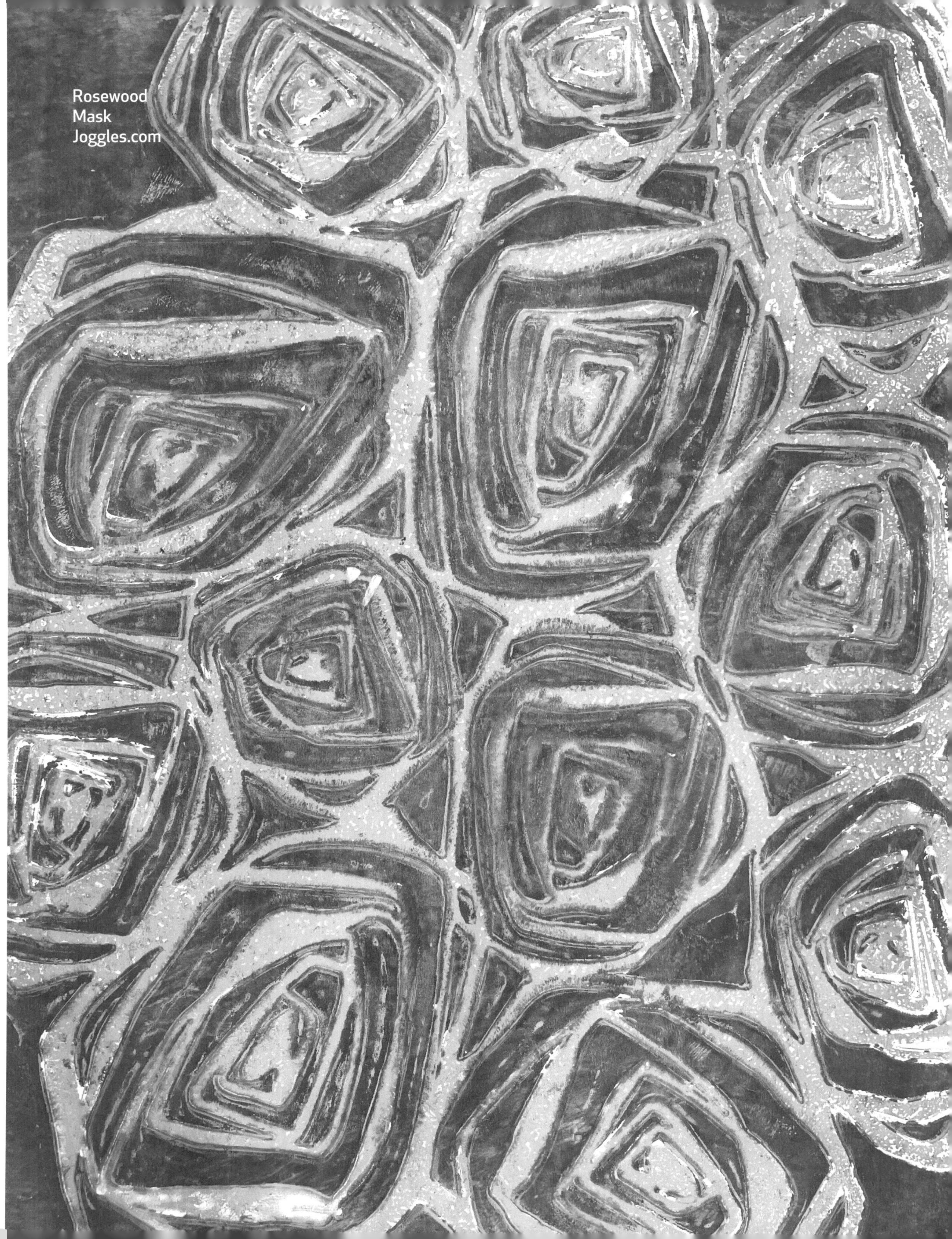
Rosewood
Mask
Joggles.com

GHOST PRINTS AND PAINT OVER STENCILS / MASKS

Another way to implement a ghost print is to leave the mask on the plate and then add a second layer paint directly over the top of the stencil. In this technique the stencil is masking out the ghost print from the second layer of paint.

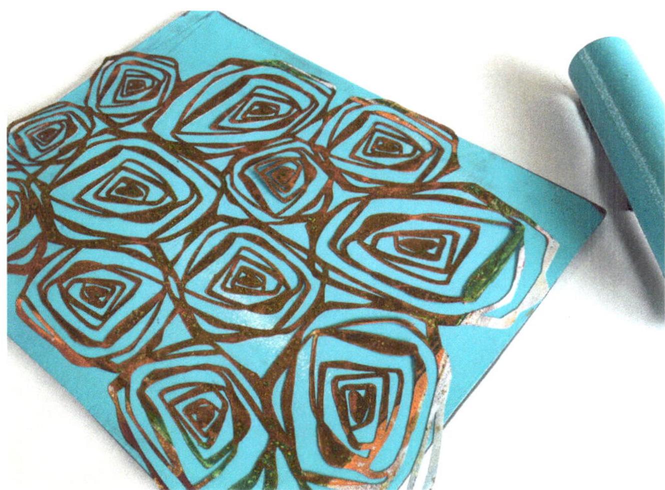

Lay the mask over a thin layer of paint (Teal) on the plate and pull a print on scrap paper in order to remove all of the paint from the negative spaces.

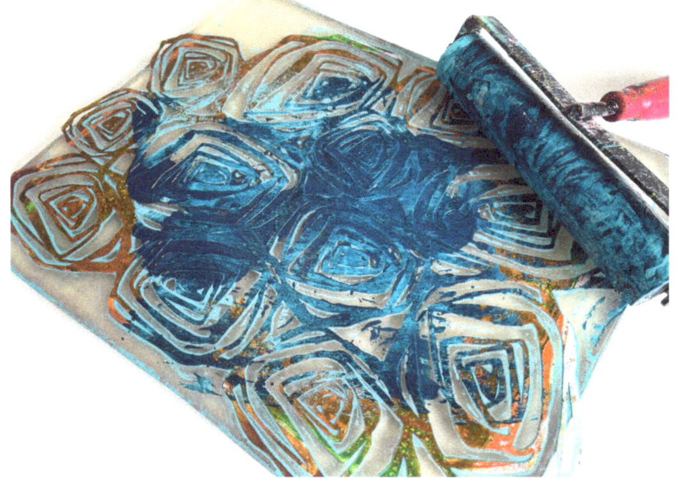

Brayer a second color (Turquoise Phthalo) OVER the mask and into the negative spaces, while it is still on the plate.

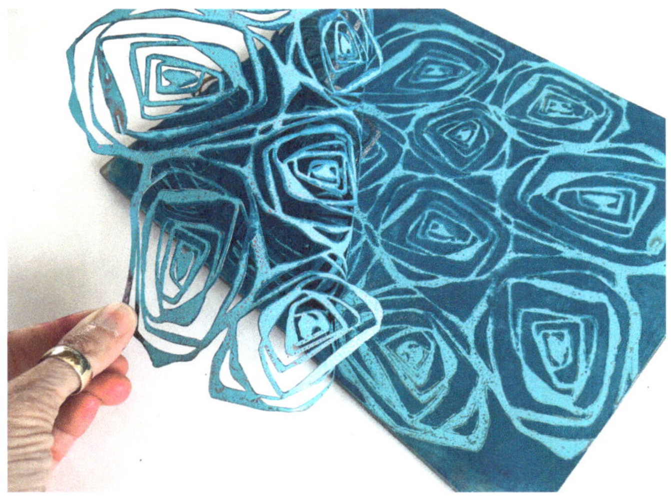

Remove the mask from the plate.

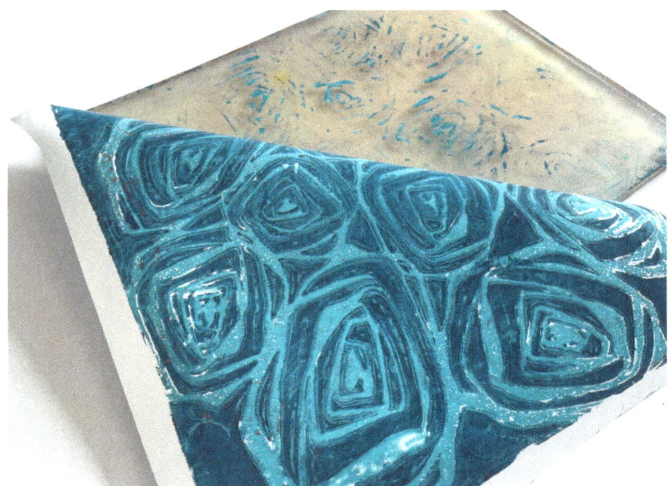

Pull both the print and the ghost print together.

ADDING WATERY WASHES TO GHOST PRINTS

Ghost prints on white rice paper look wonderful with a color wash on top. Take your Golden Fluid Acrylics, add water, and use a soft bristled brush to paint over the dry rice paper gel print. This technique produces an effect that is uniquely different from working on top of a solid base layer. Use a plastic drop cloth, shower curtain, vinyl table cloth, or a glossy palette sheet to keep the wet paper from sticking to the drying surface.

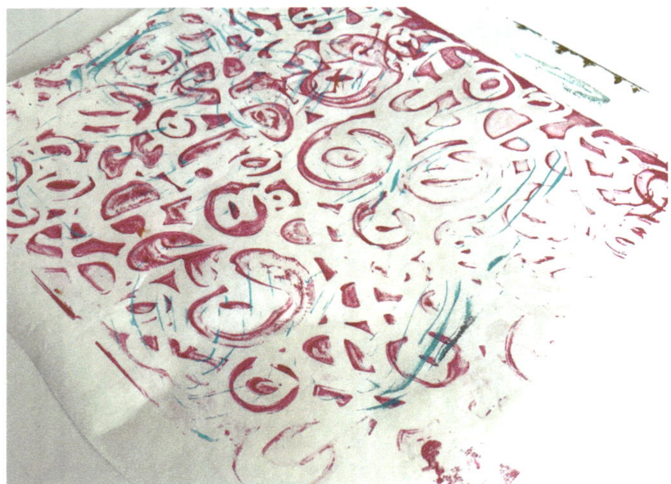

Pull a print (Quinacridone Magenta) on a scrap sheet. Transfer the ghost print to a sheet of white rice paper.

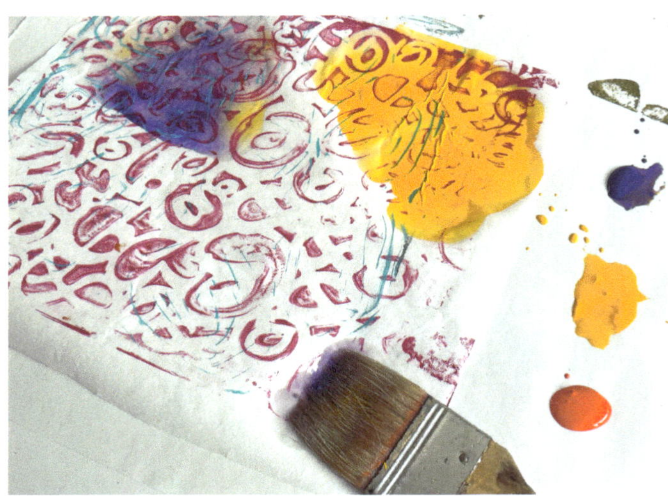

Add water to Fluid Acrylics with a soft bristled brush (Ultramarine Violet, Diarylide Yellow, Pyrolle Orange).

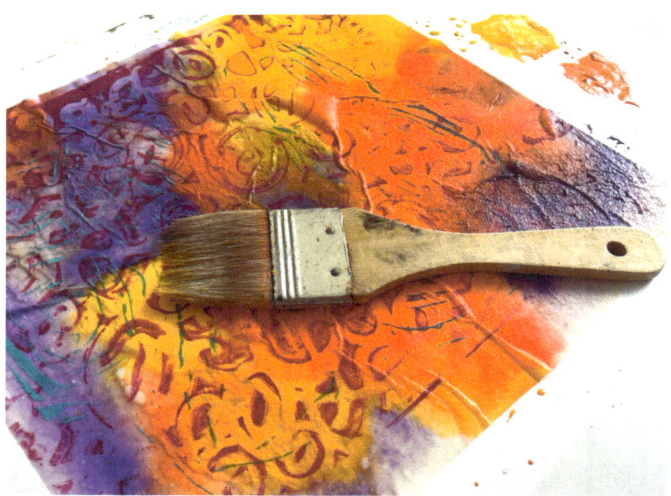

Brush the watered down color over the ghost print.

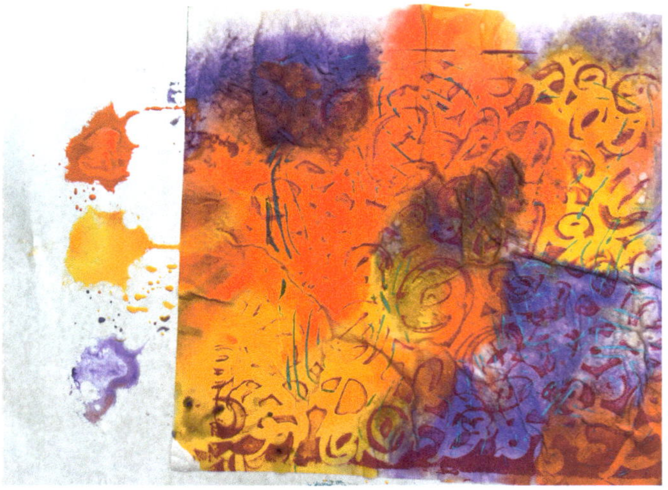

Allow the colors to blend and bleed organically.

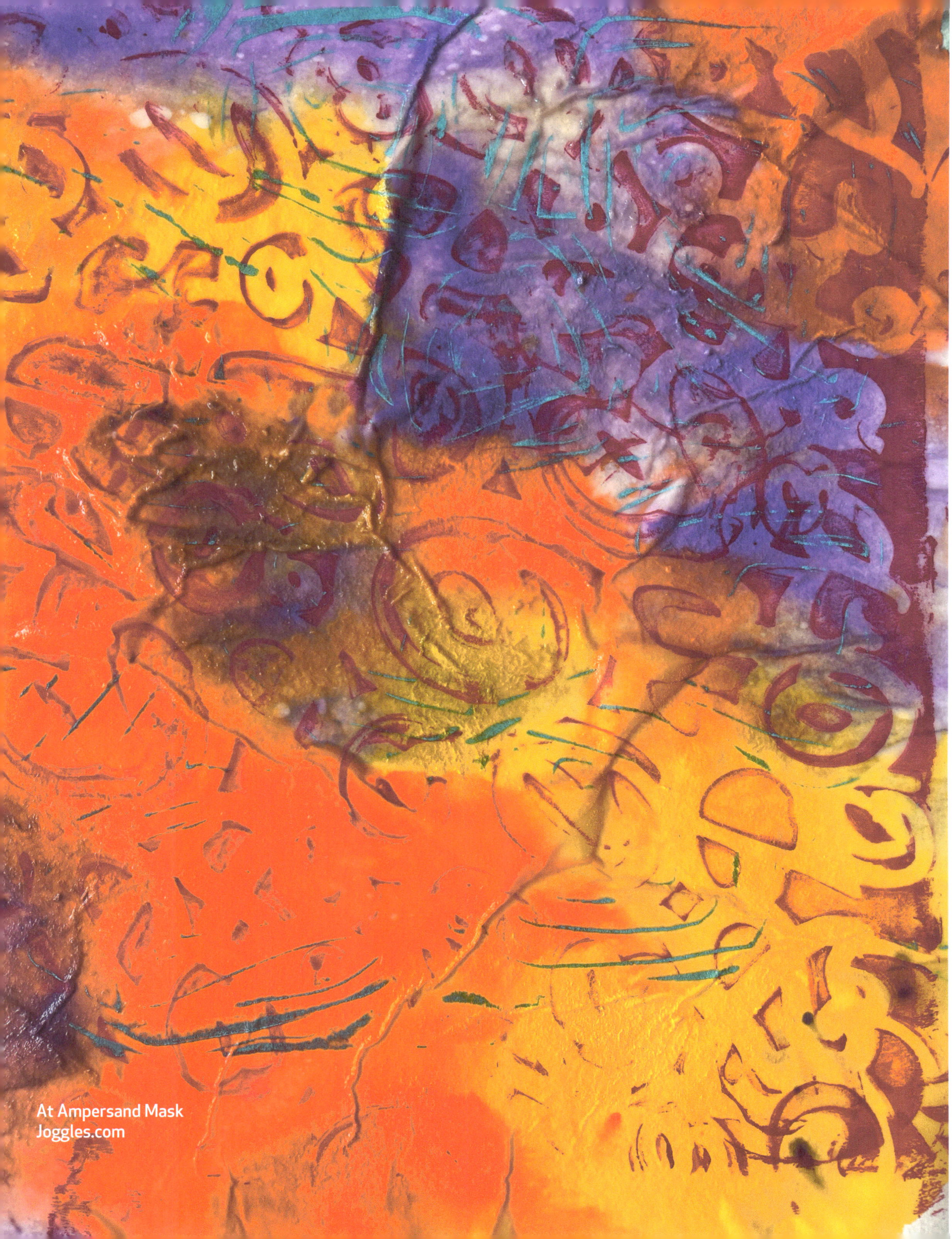
At Ampersand Mask
Joggles.com

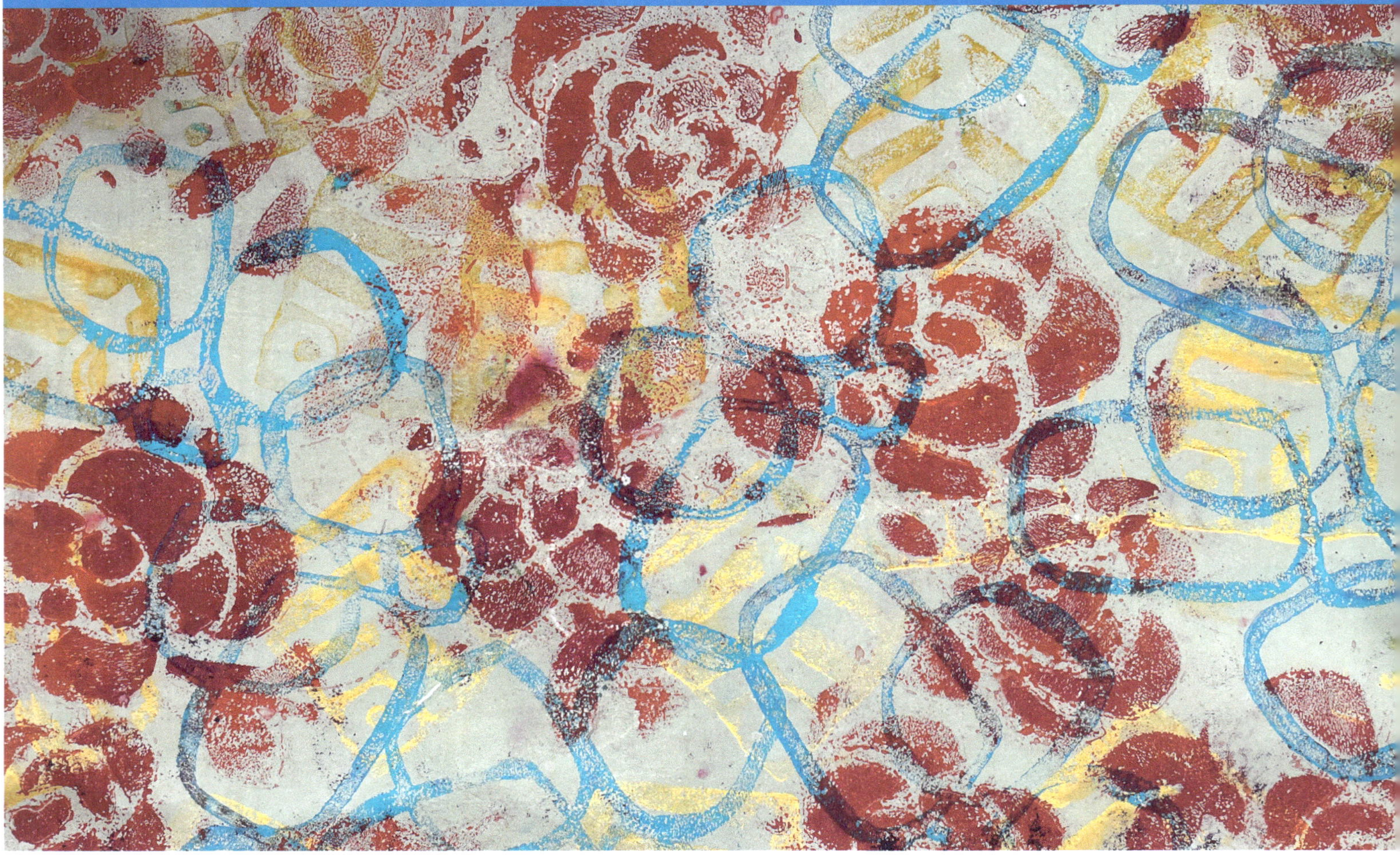

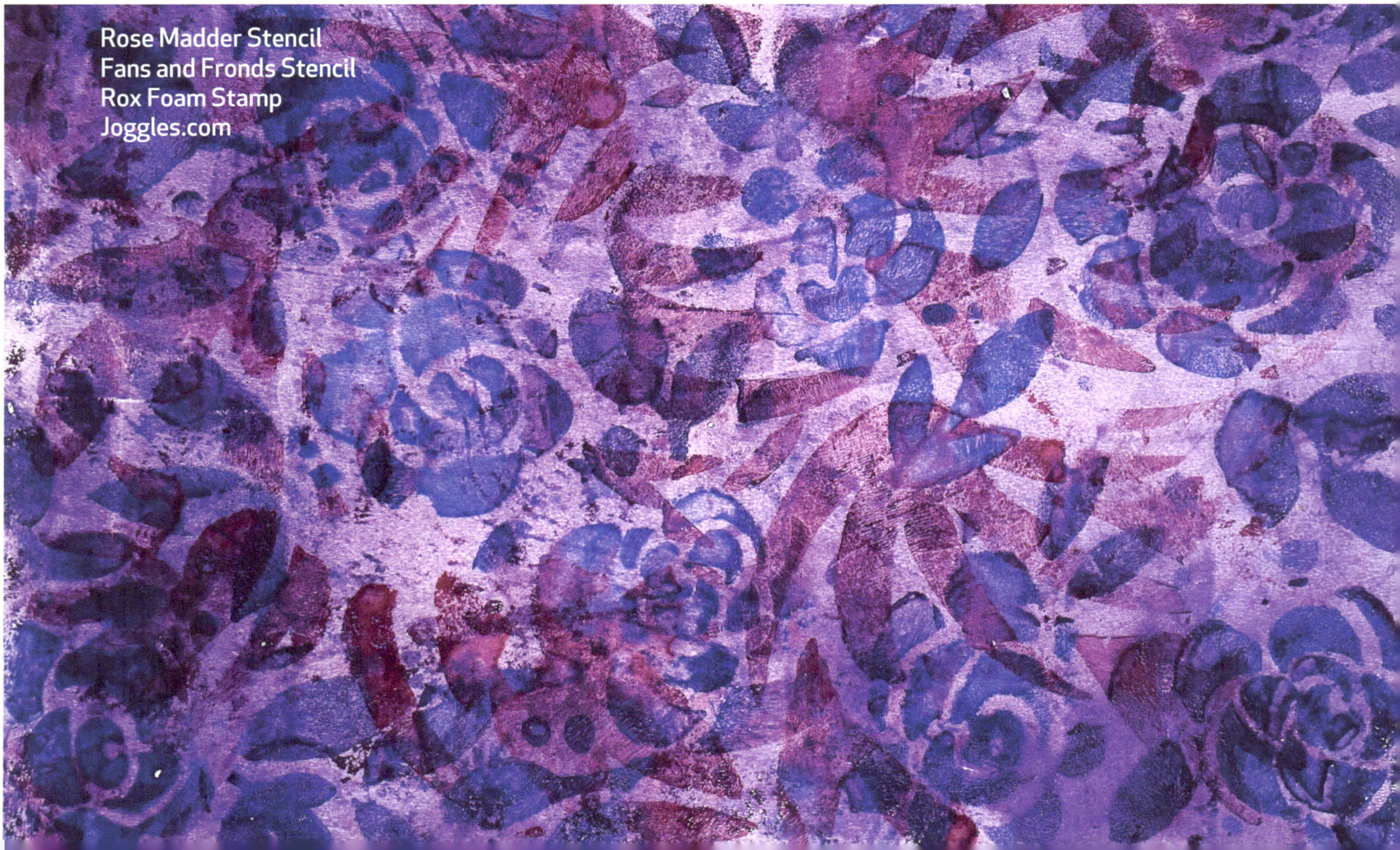

Rose Madder Stencil
Fans and Fronds Stencil
Rox Foam Stamp
Joggles.com

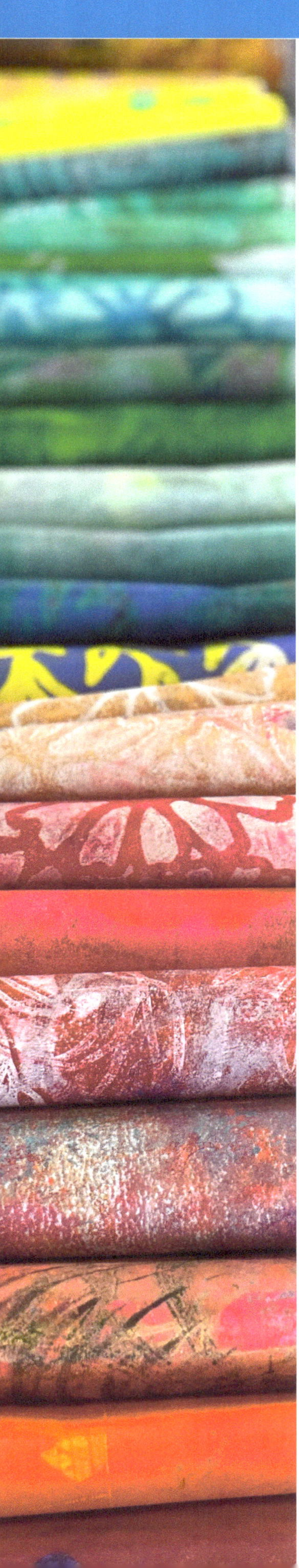

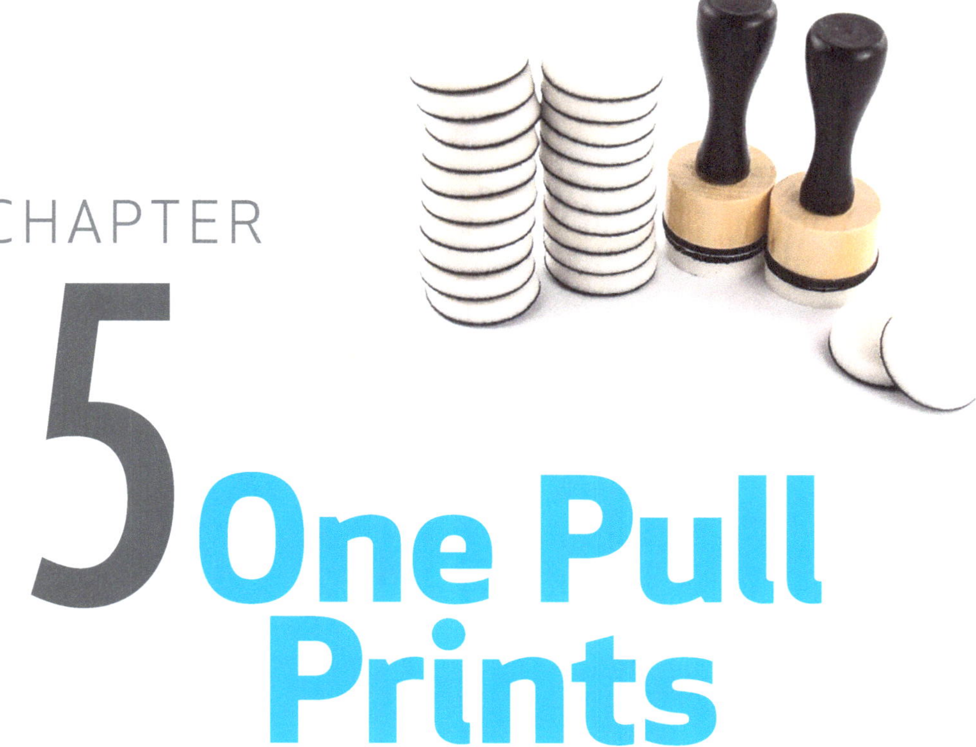

CHAPTER

5 One Pull Prints

Layers are key in gel printing but they do not always have to be created separately. One pull prints allow time for you to curate your colors, textures, and patterns on the plate before you pull your final print with a layer of paint over the top. I use the Mini Ink Blending tool to dab color through specific sections of the stencil directly onto the plate. I also incorporate some stamps for more complex, layered prints.

When you apply a fresh layer of wet paint over the top of all the dried paint on the plate, it will cause the plate to release all your layers in one pull. These prints can be tons of fun and often offer unexpected results!

DABBING PAINT THROUGH A STENCIL

Create all your patterns and textures directly onto the plate using a dabbing tool such as Ranger's Mini Ink Blender to apply paint through selective sections of stencils and masks in different colors.

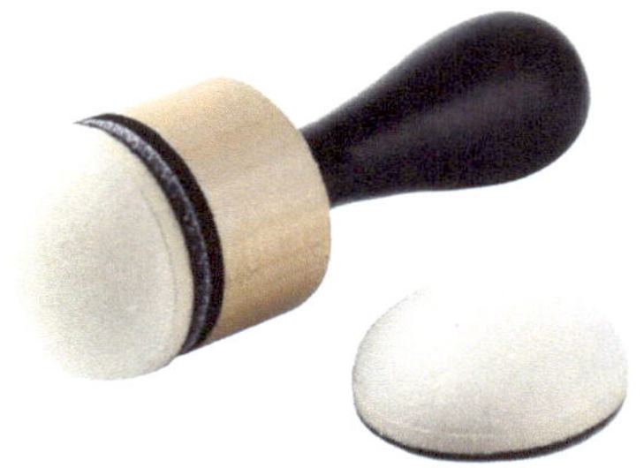

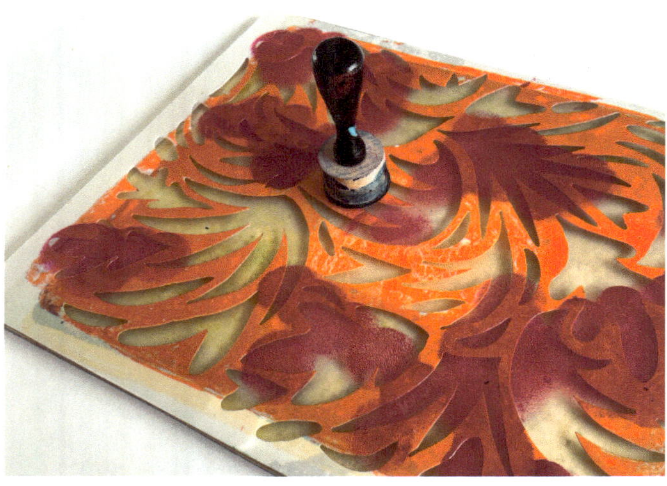

Place a stencil on the clean gel plate. Dab color (Quin Magenta) through parts of the stencil in random areas, covering about 20% of the plate, leaving open spaces.

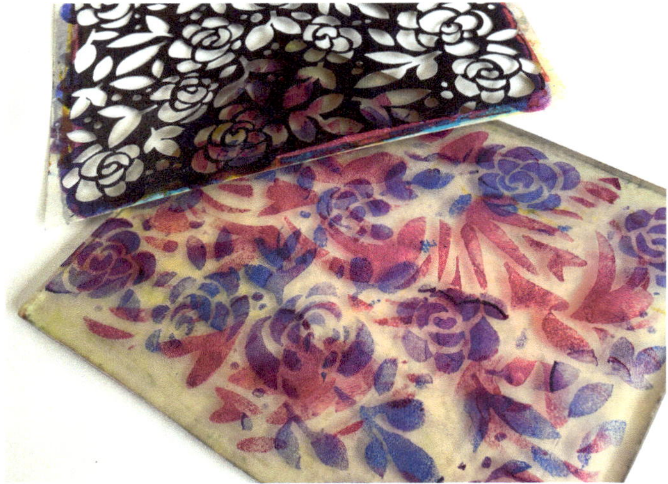

Come in with a second color (Ultramarine Blue) and second stencil pattern and dab through again covering another 20% and leaving some open spaces. Remove the stencil.

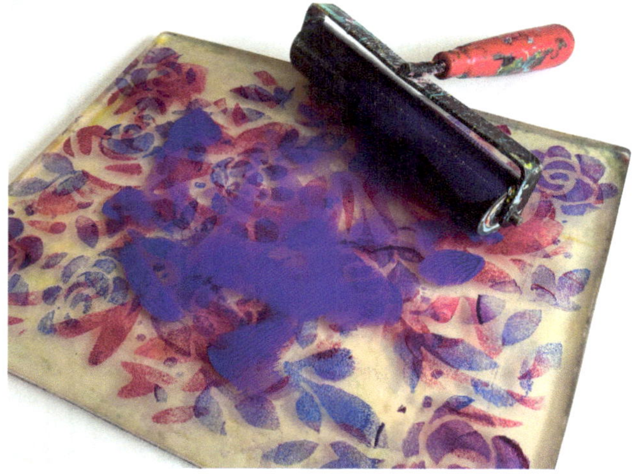

When dry, spread a color (Ultramarine Violet) that is lighter or darker in value over the whole plate.

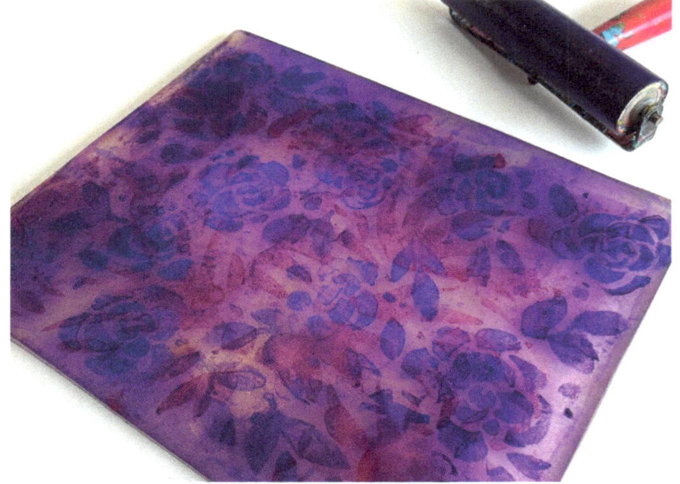

Pull the one pull print.

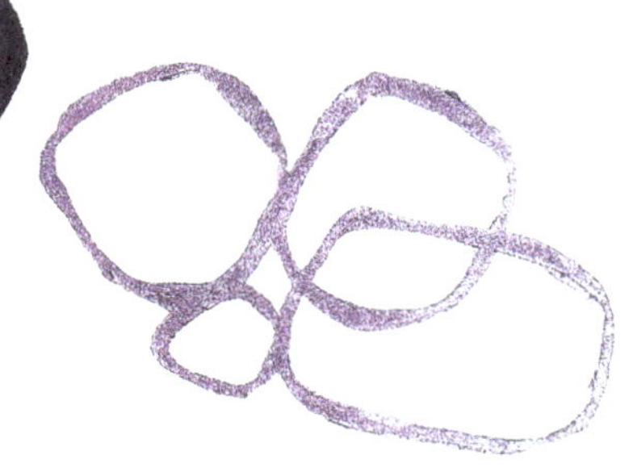

ADDING STAMPING TO THE MIX

Once you get the hang of dabbing paint through parts of a stencil onto the plate, try incorporating some stamping and directly onto the plate in combination with the partial stencil impressions.
Below: Rox Foam Stamp for Joggles.com

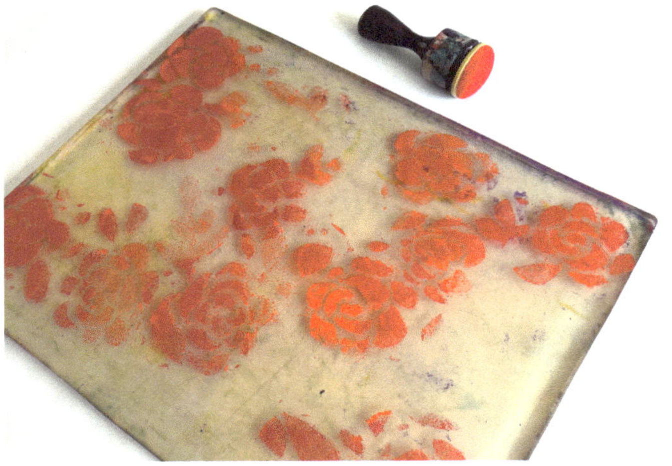

Place a stencil on the clean plate. Dab color through parts of the stencil in random areas, covering about 20% of the plate, leaving open spaces. (Pyrolle Red and Orange)

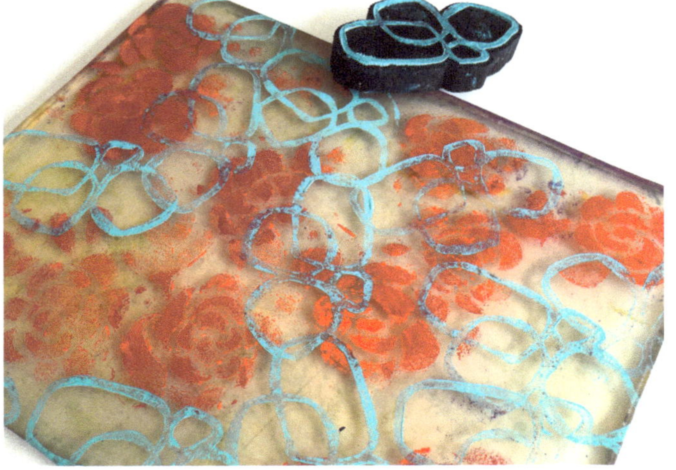

Add a contrasting paint color (Teal) to the stamp with a small two inch brayer and stamp into about 20% of the open spaces.

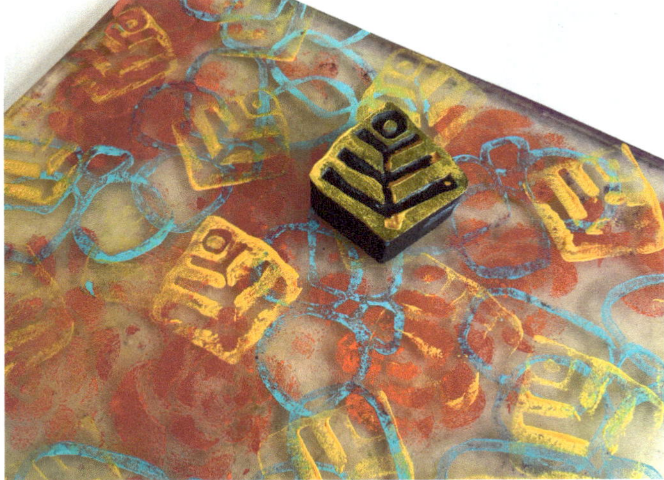

Let the paint dry and bring in a second stamp with a contrasting color (Bright Gold Fine) and stamp again into about 20% of the open spaces.

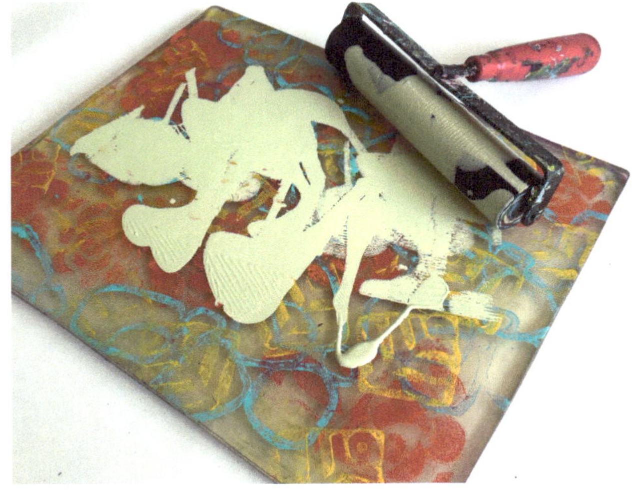

Cover the plate with a contrasting paint color (Titan Green Pale) and pull the print. ***NOTE: wash paint from stamps immediately to avoid drying on and ruining the surface of the foam.***

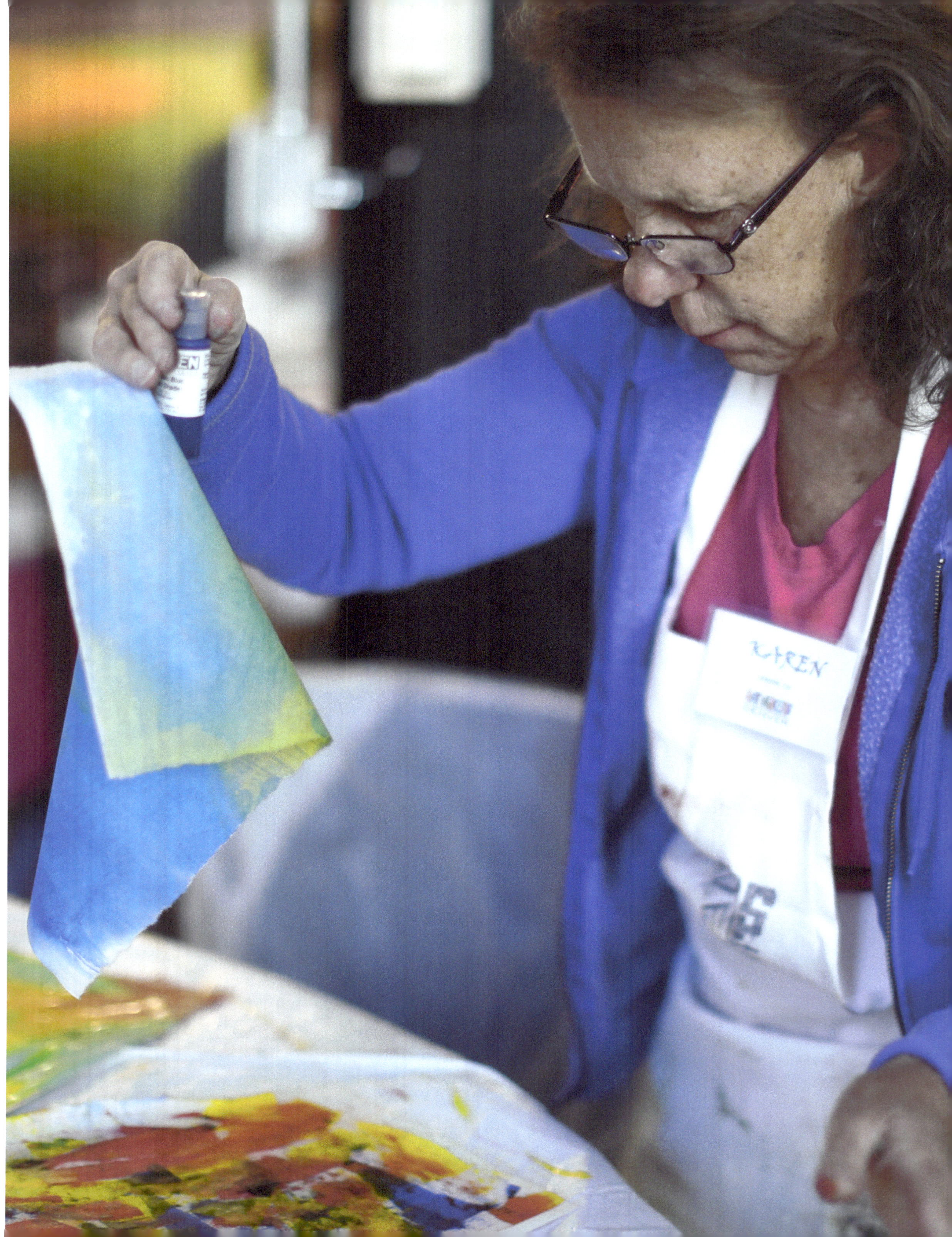

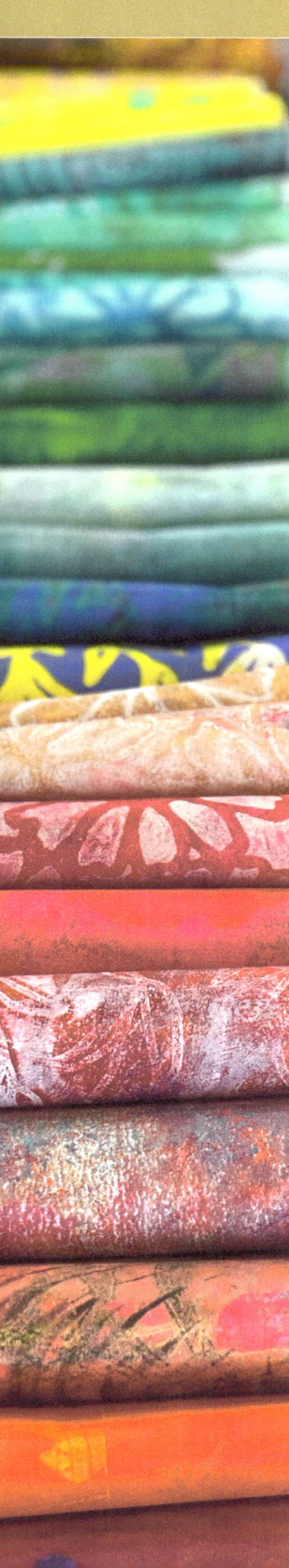

CHAPTER

6 After Effects

Once you have created some fun prints, you can add more interest to them with some additional off-the-plate techniques. Let's kick this up a notch!

When using rice paper I like to soak paint through the back side of the paper for interesting effects and to create colored edges when tearing.

Want to add a little pizazz? Consider adding a bit of glittery goodness or paint pens to the mix.

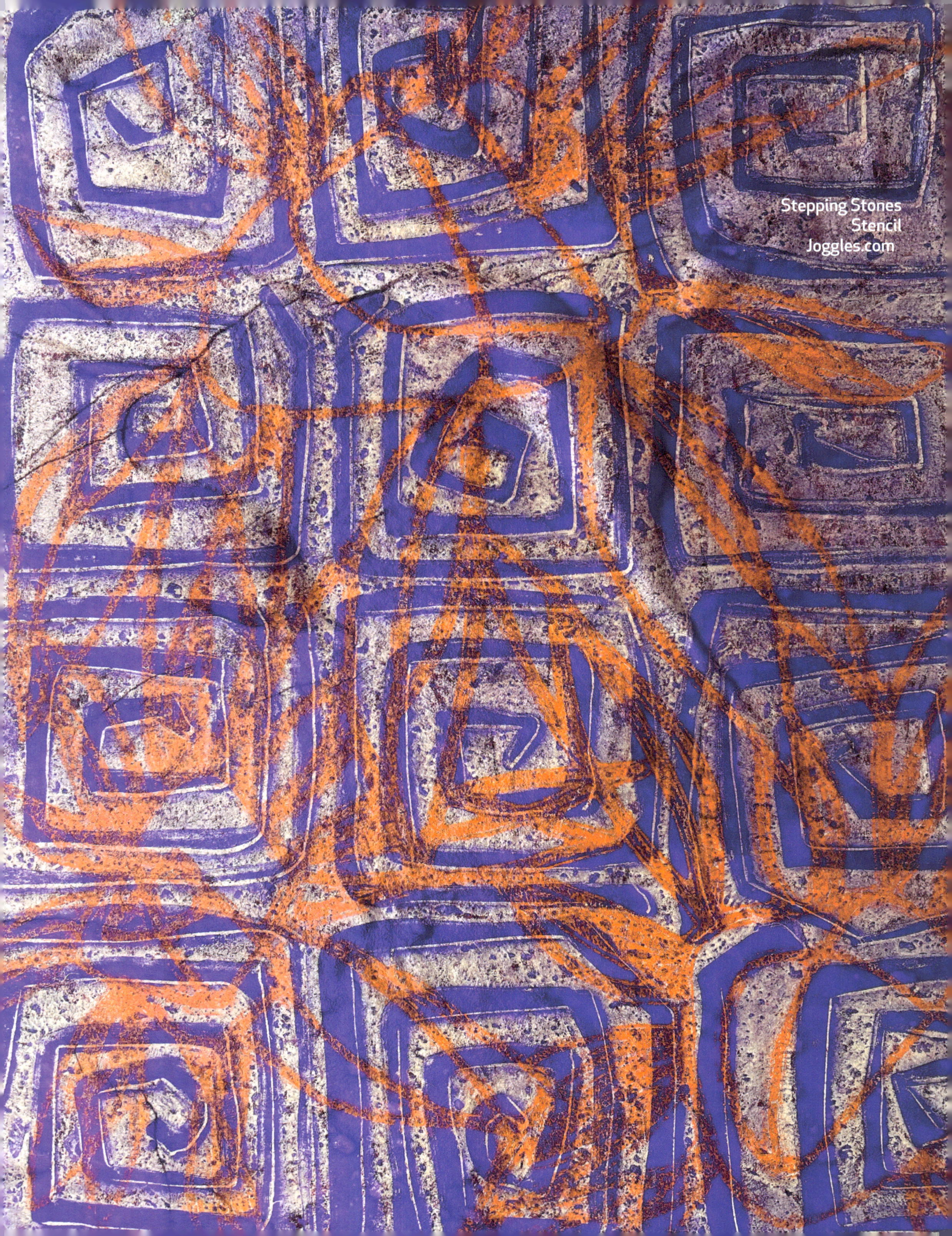

Stepping Stones
Stencil
Joggles.com

SOAKING COLOR THROUGH THE BACK

With rice paper you can soak color through the back of your prints, creating the unique effect of colored edges when torn, which is wonderful if you are using your papers in collage. This technique only works with rice paper as it is highly absorbent. Use a plastic drop cloth, shower curtain, vinyl table cloth, or a glossy palette sheet to keep the wet paper from sticking to the drying surface. Below: *Deconstructed Daisies mask for Joggles.com*

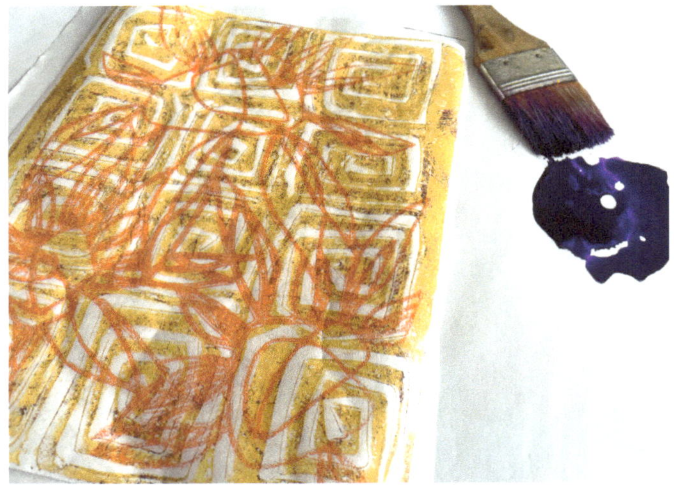

Take a layered gel print you have created (Naples Yellow, Pyrolle Orange) on white rice paper and spread out a contrasting color (Dioxazine Purple) with water.

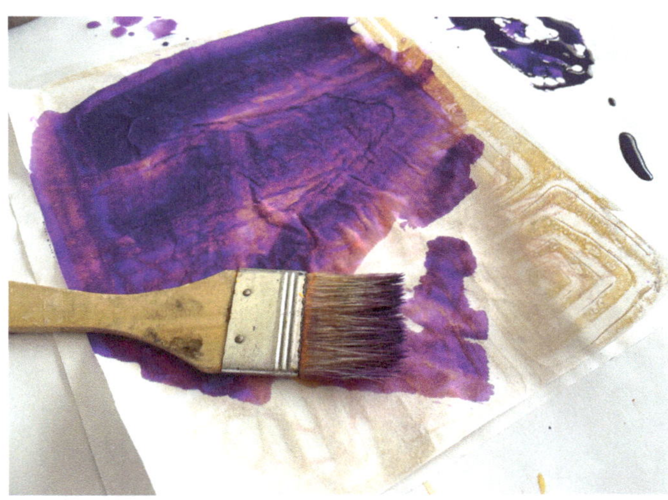

Flip over your rice paper print and apply a watery wash of color to soak all the way through the paper.

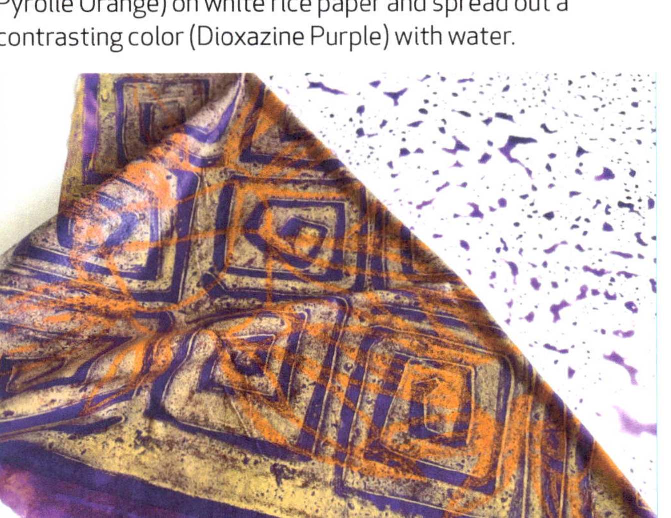

The purple does not totally mute the yellow because it is soaking through the rice paper from the back versus being applied on top.

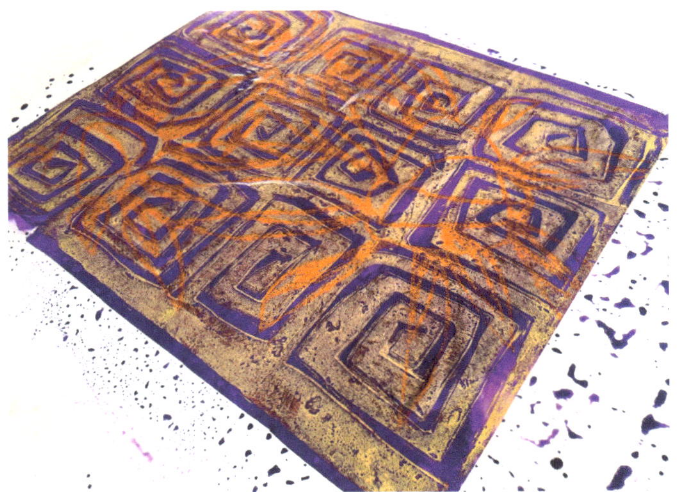

Allow the paper to dry completely before peeling away from the plastic.

EMBELLISHING WITH SPLATTER

One of my favorite effects is adding a little splatter on top of a richly layered gel print. I love the way the little dots are like a cherry on top of a beautiful print. Be sure to use opaque or metallic colors that will stand out on your last layer. Gold, Bronze, Copper, and/or Teal are always a big hit with any color combination.

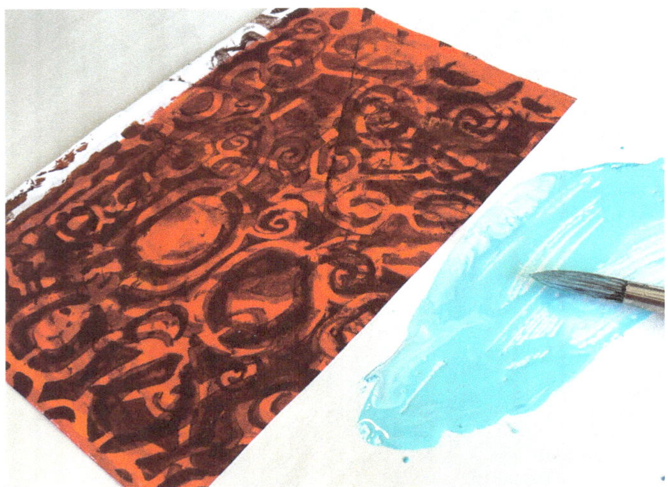

Add water to a color that contrasts with your print (Teal with Titanium White).

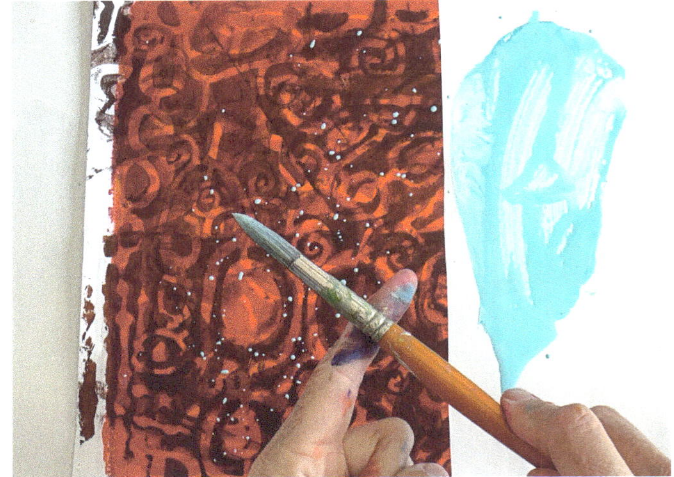

Tap the paint-filled brush against your finger to control the splatter.

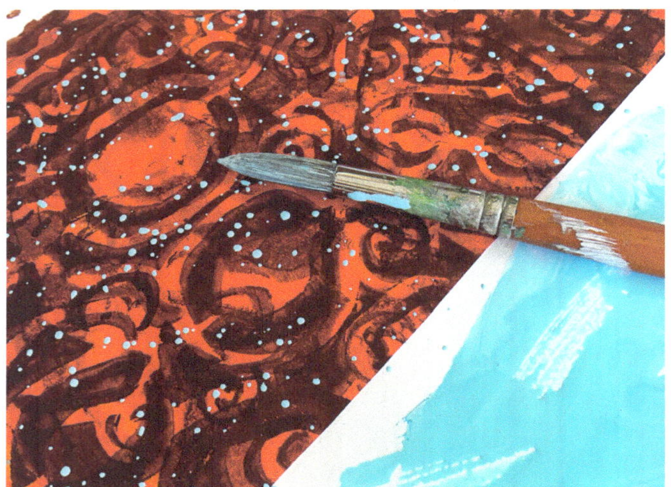

Opaque Teal stands out nicely even against the darkest tones in this print.

TIP: More water makes bigger splats, less water makes smaller dots. Experiment with how far away you are when you tap the brush, and how fast or how slow you tap. You can also squeeze the bristles of the brush to create large splats or fling the brush for splatter that appears in a line. Experiment with mixing metallic paint into other colors of fluid acrylics to create a paint that will stand out over the top of darker colors but is not limited to Gold, Bronze, or Copper. Quinacridone Magenta looks glorious when mixed with Gold Metallic, just sayin'.

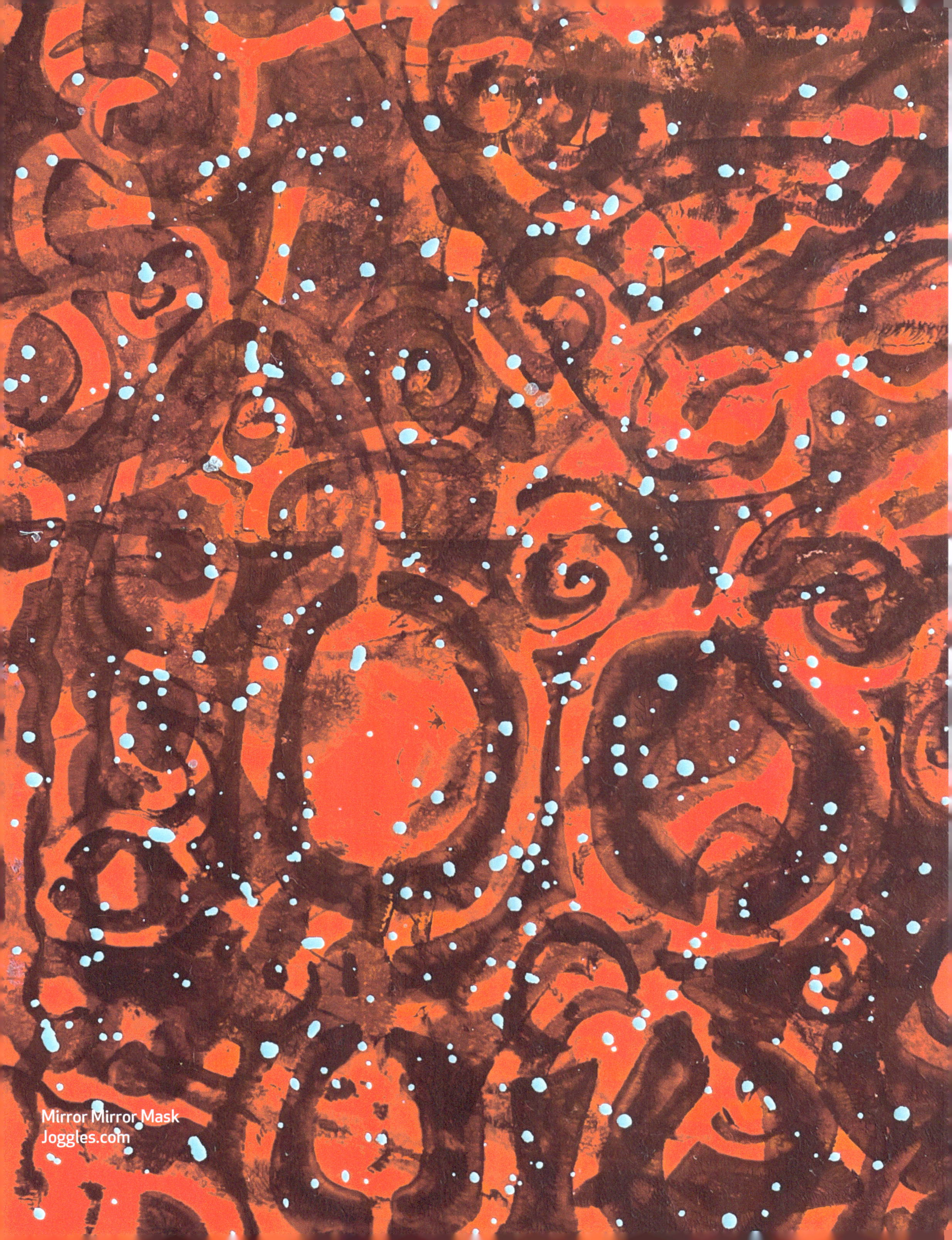
Mirror Mirror Mask
Joggles.com

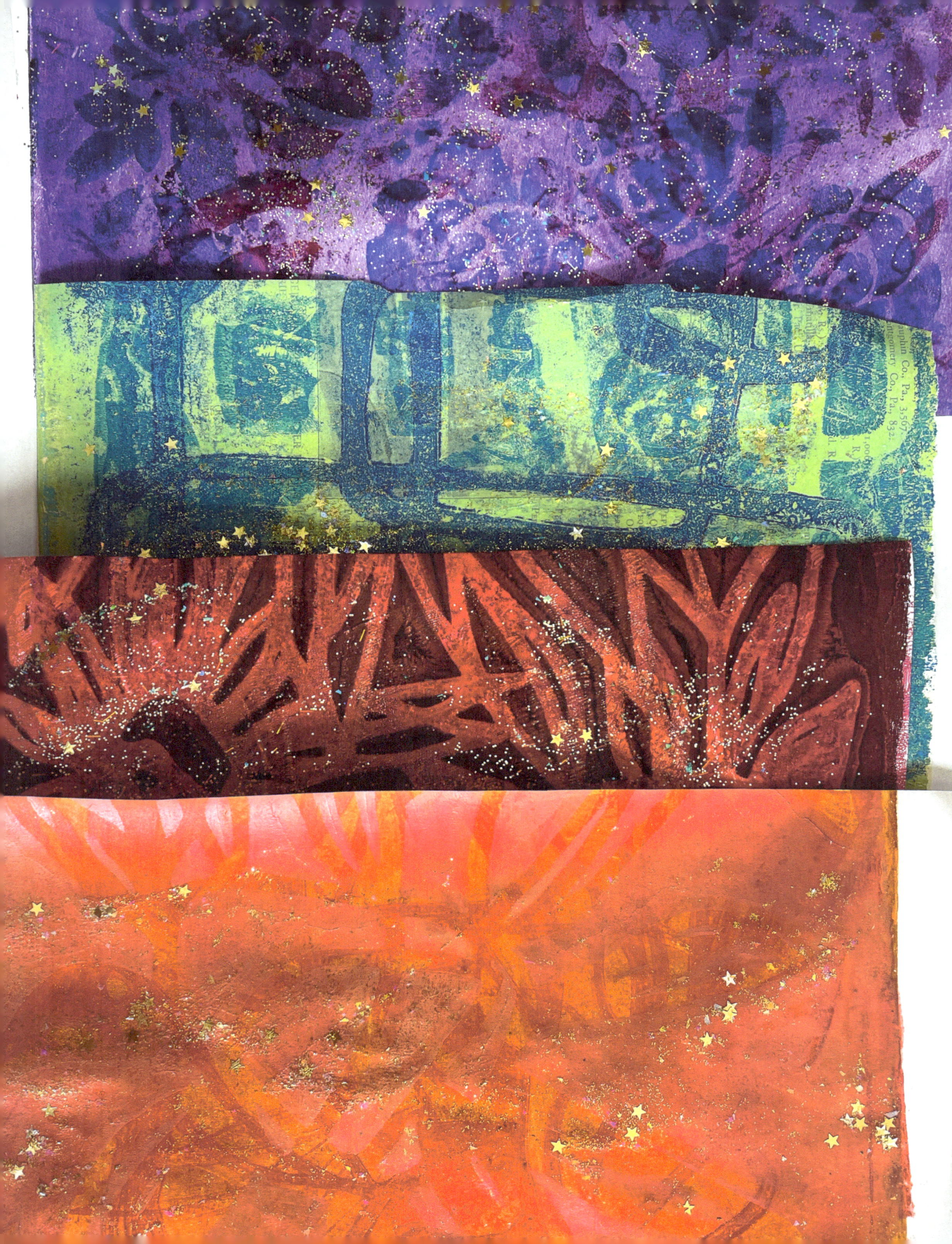

INCORPORATING GLITTER

While working with glitter can be messy, it's still a favorite–who doesn't love a little bling?
Glitter can be SUPER tricky to clean up when you use it by shaking into glue. An alternative to loose glitter, Ranger makes a product called Stickles Glitter Gel that has chunky, fun glitter shapes suspended in gel. Spread it over your prints with a palette knife and add a no-mess pizazz that will take your prints to another level!

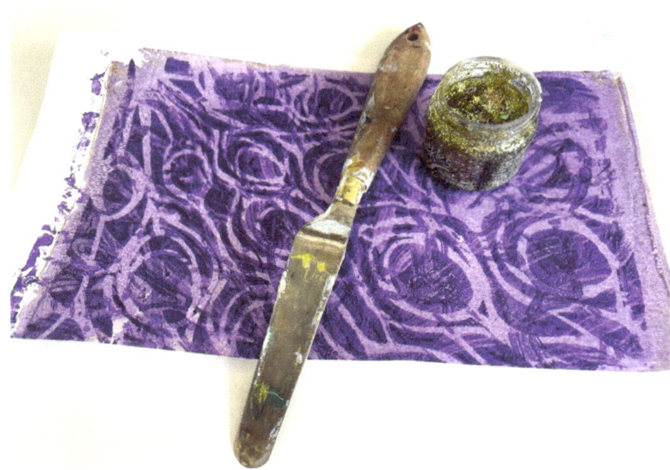

Take a layered gel print you have created. Use a palette knife to scoop the glitter out of the container and spread.

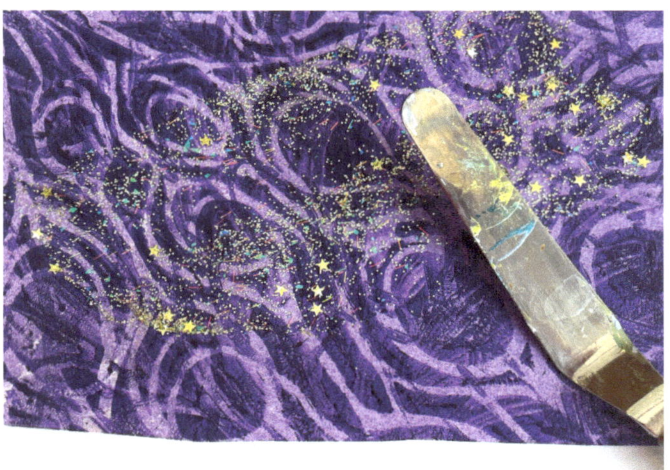

Scrape the palette knife to disperse a thin layer of the glitter gel and to expose the large chunky glitter shapes.

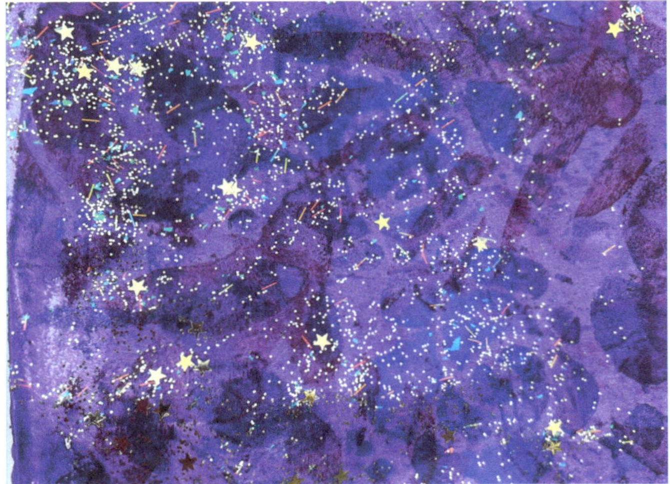

Gold is a nice choice for this dark purple sheet because it is lighter and offers high contrast in value and color. .

TIP: The gitter suspended in this glue gel does not brush off once the product is dried. There is no messy clean up of loose glitter, and no glitter has to go down the drain into the water supply. Simply wipe the product off your tools and surface with a paper towel, allow it to dry, and throw it into the trash–it's that simple!

Joggles.com stocks Stickles Glitter Gel in many color options that feature some different chunky glitter shapes.

GOING DUTCH

In order to achieve more visual variety in your gel prints, consider splitting them in half and adding one more layer to just half of the sheet. An additional layer of effects can take one half of the paper in a total different direction. In this example I am taking one half of the sheet down to a much darker value, utilizing the existing patterns and textures on the original print.

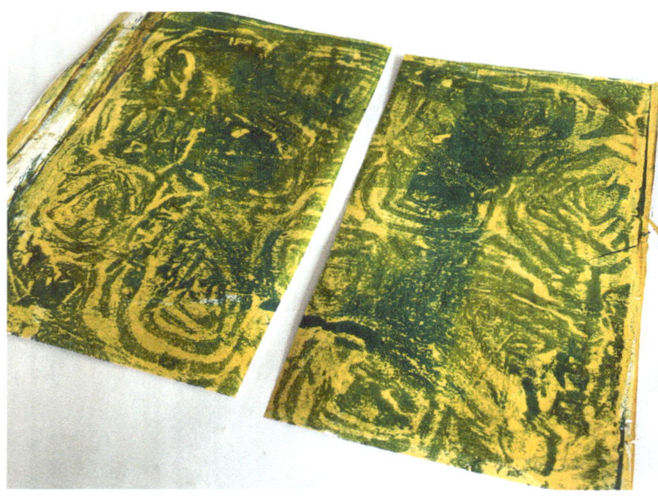

Take a finished print and divide it in half. Keep half the original color (Green Gold and Sap Green) and make half darker with another layer.

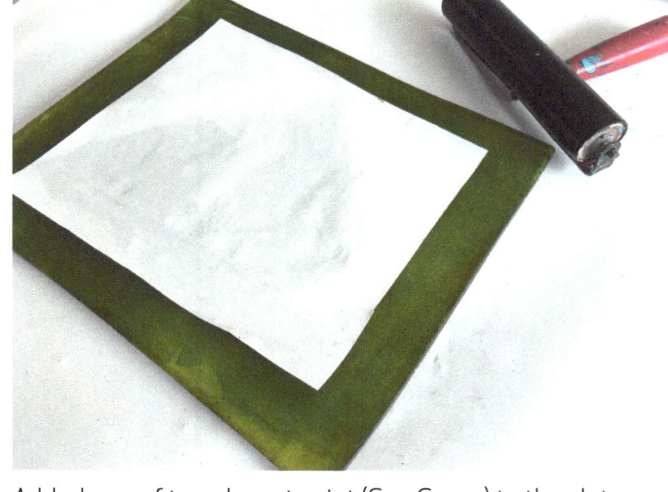

Add a layer of translucent paint (Sap Green) to the plate that is slightly darker and put one half of the original print into the color.

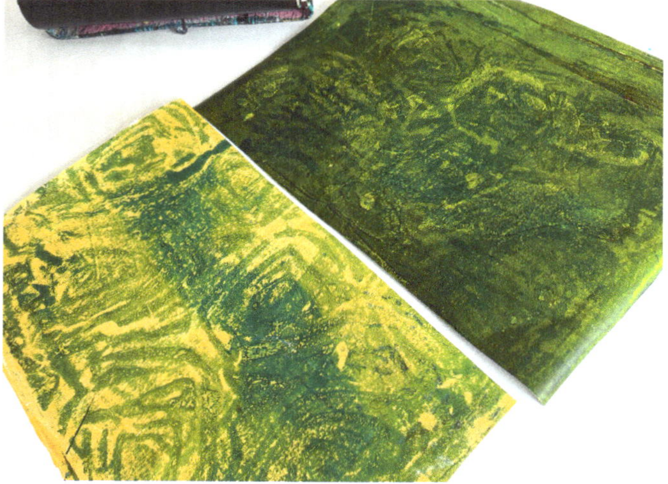

Pull the print.

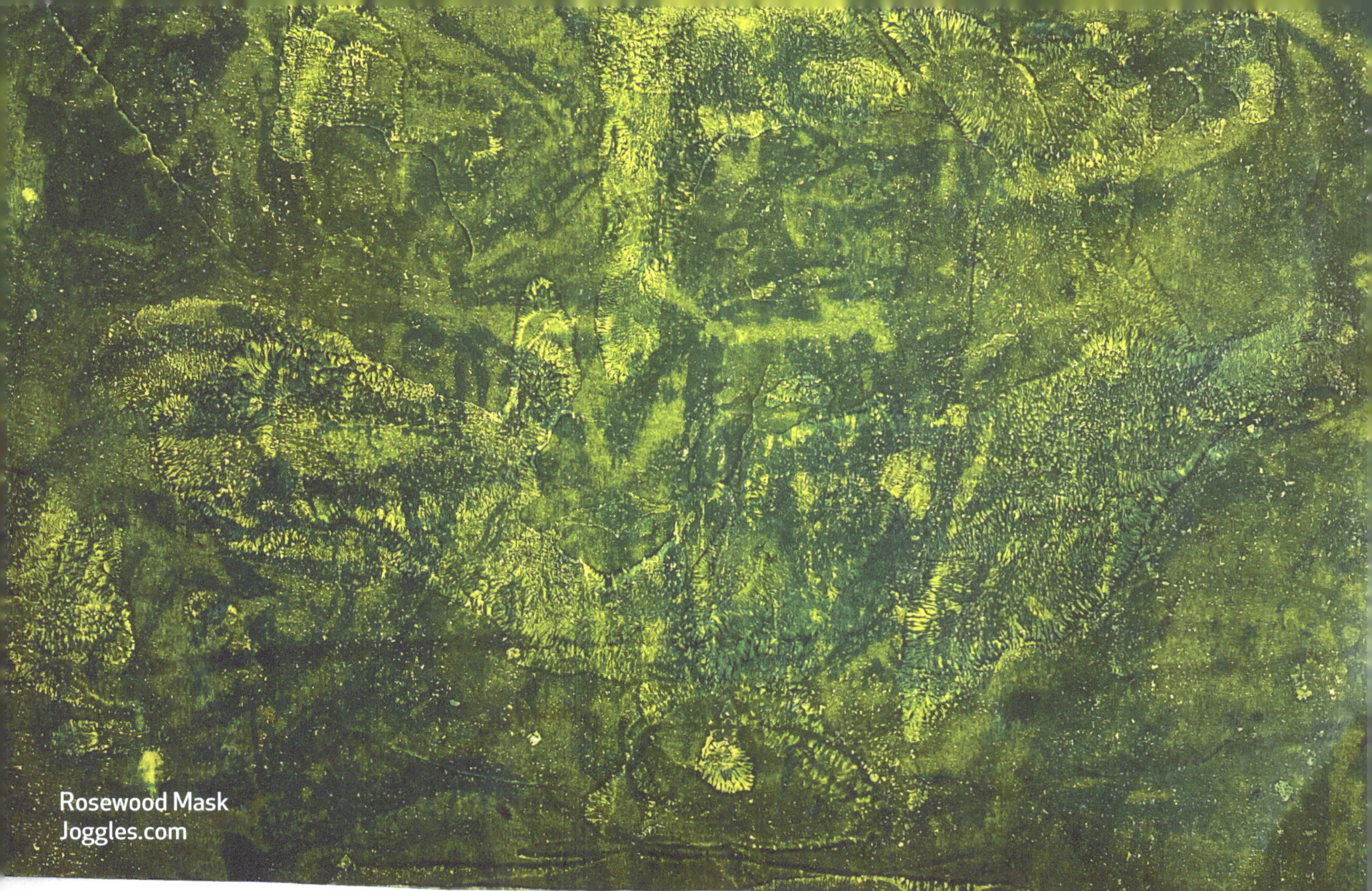

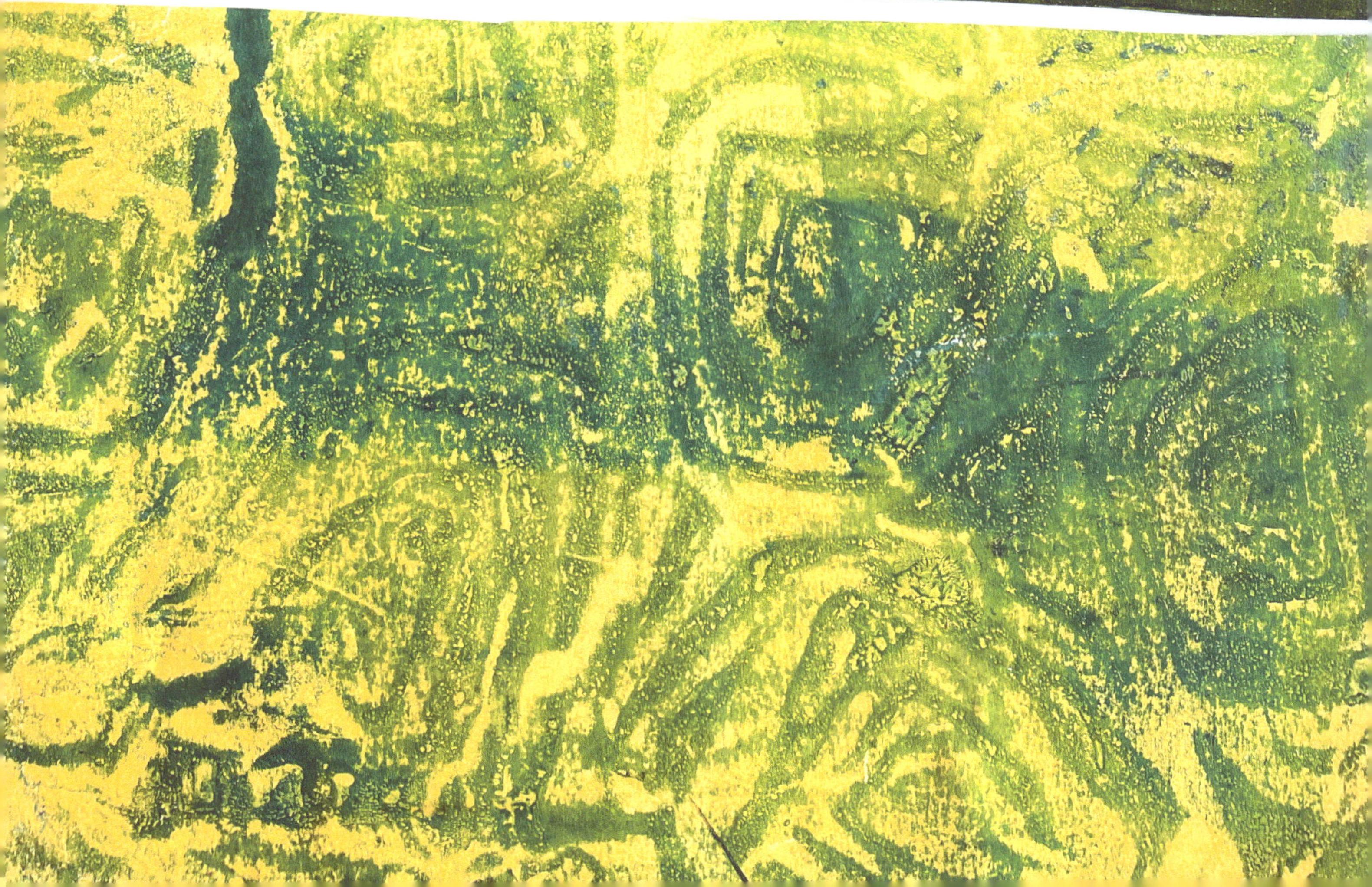

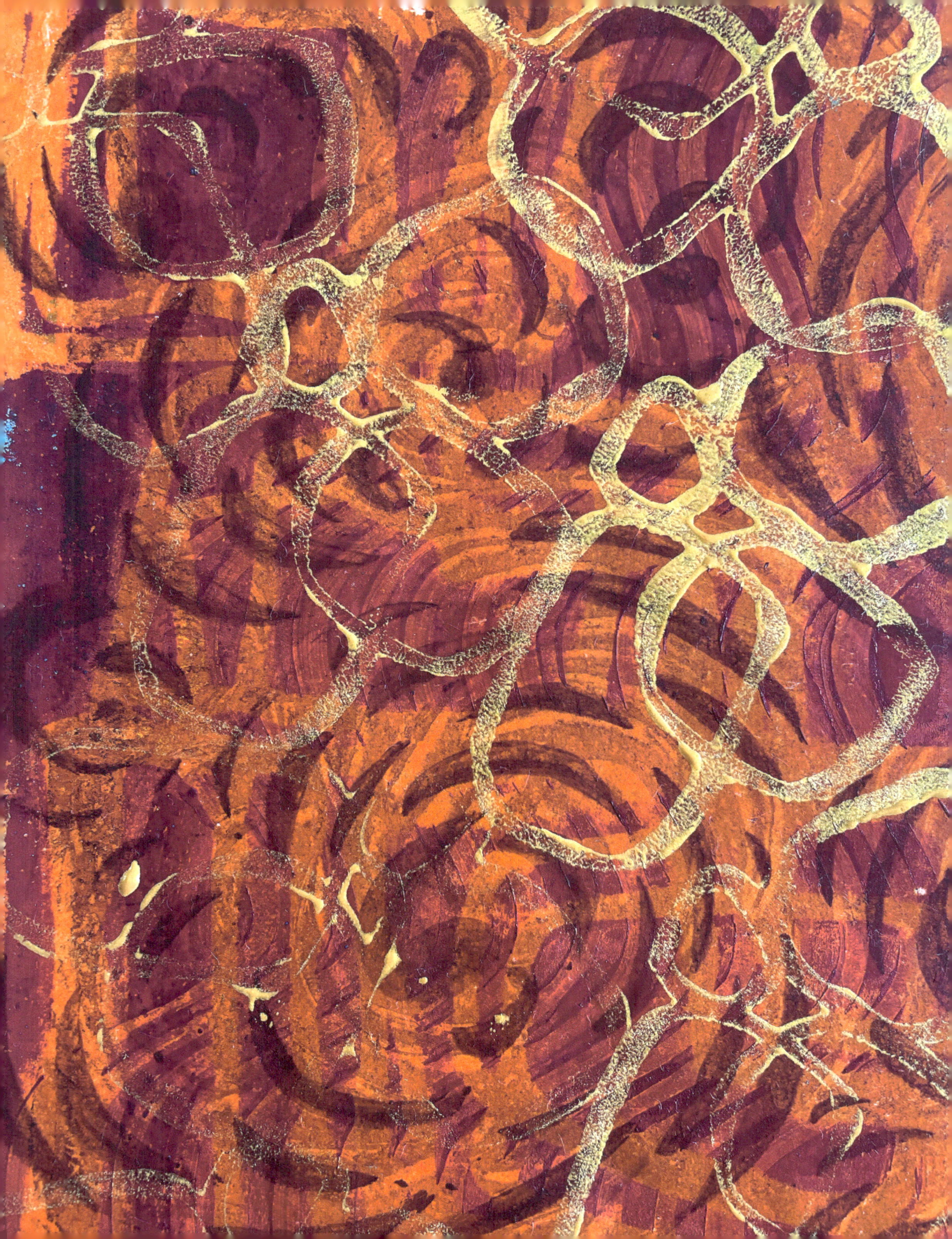

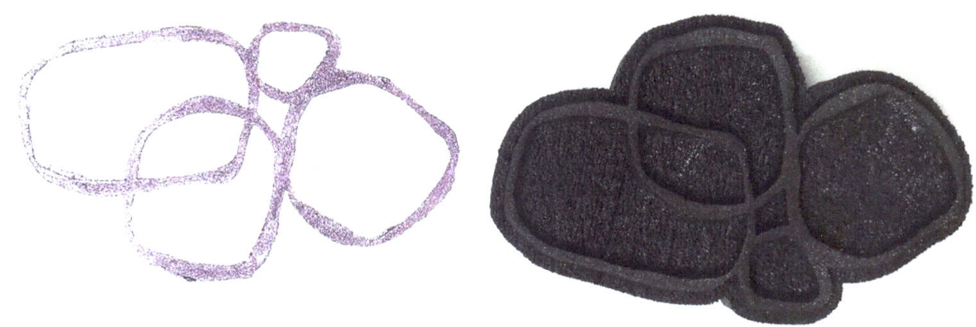

STAMPING ON TOP

While I love to incorporate stamps into the print, I also enjoy adding a final layer of stamped pattern on top of my gel prints for a little more pizazz. When stamping on top I use metallic or opaque color that will show up easily over my previous layers; a darker color can also work if you have not gone too dark in your print.
Below: Rox foam stamp design for Joggles.com.

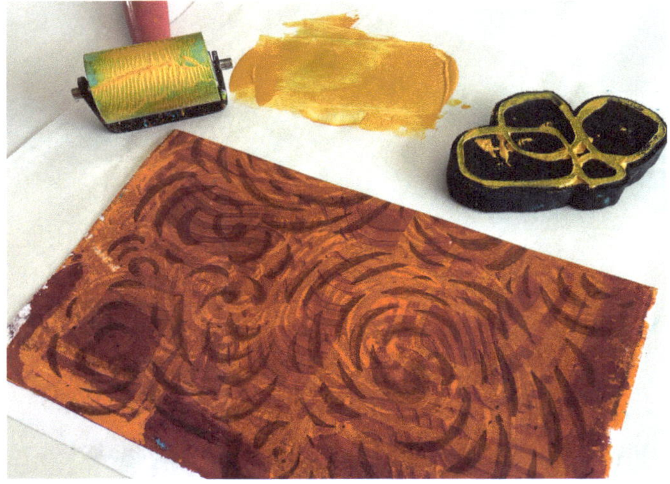

Take a print and divide it in half to add an additional effect. (Pyrolle Orange, Magenta, Van Dyke Brown).

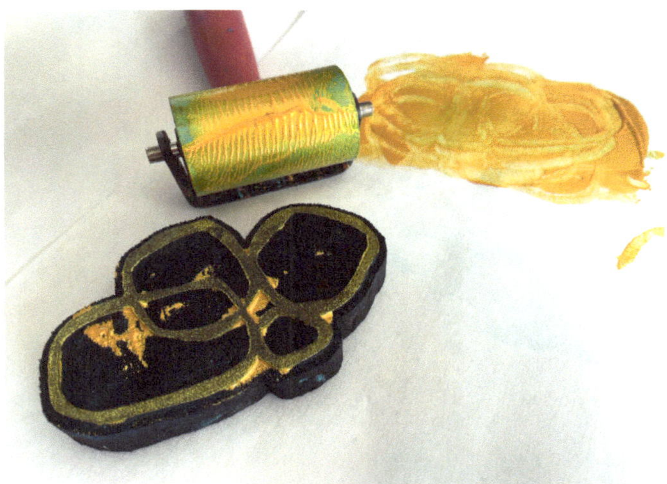

Apply a contrasting paint color (Bright Gold Fine) to a foam stamp with a two-inch brayer and stamp it over your layered gel print.

TIP: Be sure to clean the surface of your foam stamps completely from arylic paint before it dries or it will ruin the surface. Put them immediately face-down into the warm soapy water of your dish basin, wipe them with wet paper towels or baby wipes, or wash them with the Scrubby soap bar (this works wonders).

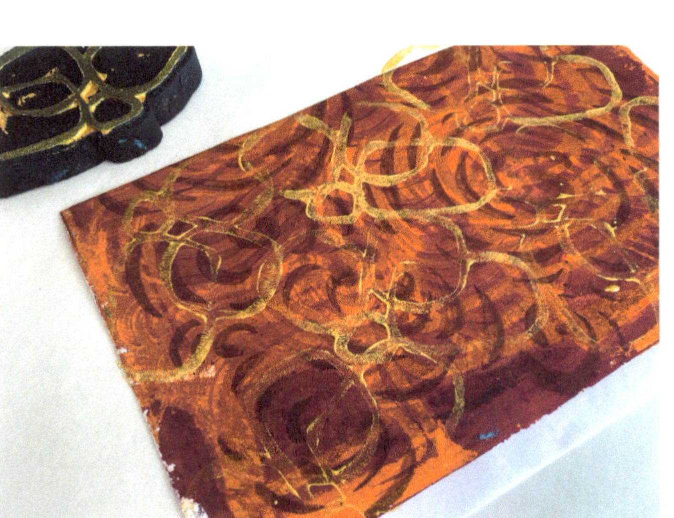

Stamp overlapping and intersecting, changing the direction of your stamp as you transfer the gold paint to your print.

MARK MAKING

Adding lines and marks, dashes and dots, X's and O's in your own hand adds a personal touch to your gel prints. Try scribbling with materials such as paint markers, micron pens, wax crayons, etc. Random hand-drawn patterns can be difficult to keep loose–experiment by incorporating your non dominant hand in order to be more spontaneous with your line.

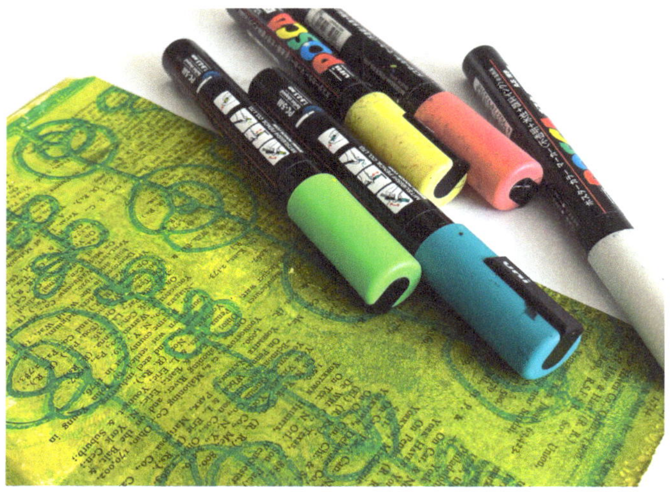

Take a finished print and divide it in half. Use Posca Paint Pens or a similar opaque markers to draw on top.

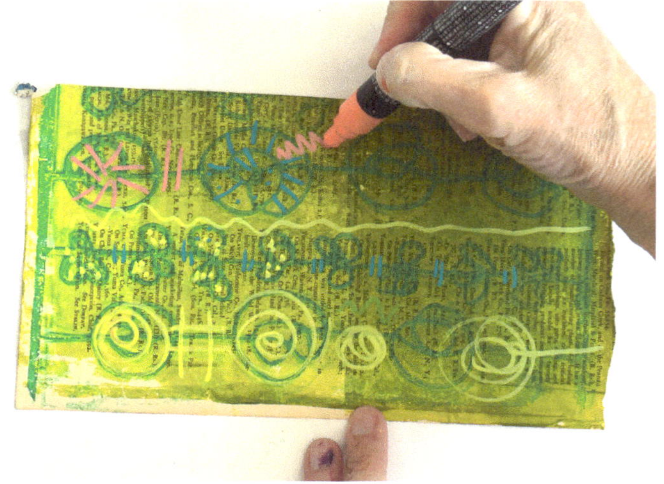

Trace the stencil lines, create your own marks, doodle with different colors and experiment with your other hand.

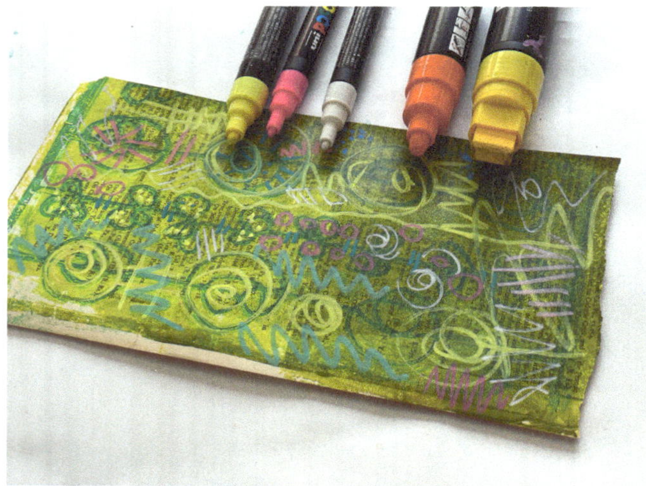

Poscas come in many different nibs, colors, metallics, and glitter varieties–they are wonderful for playing.

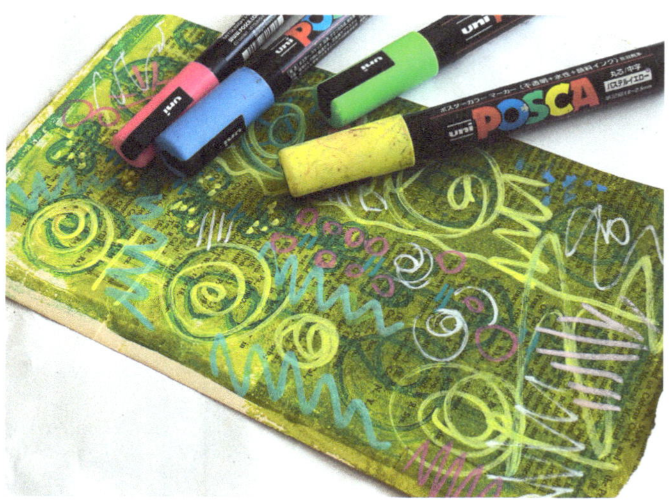

Experiment with tracing and embellishing the mask pattern, scribbling, scratching, drawing, doodling, etc.

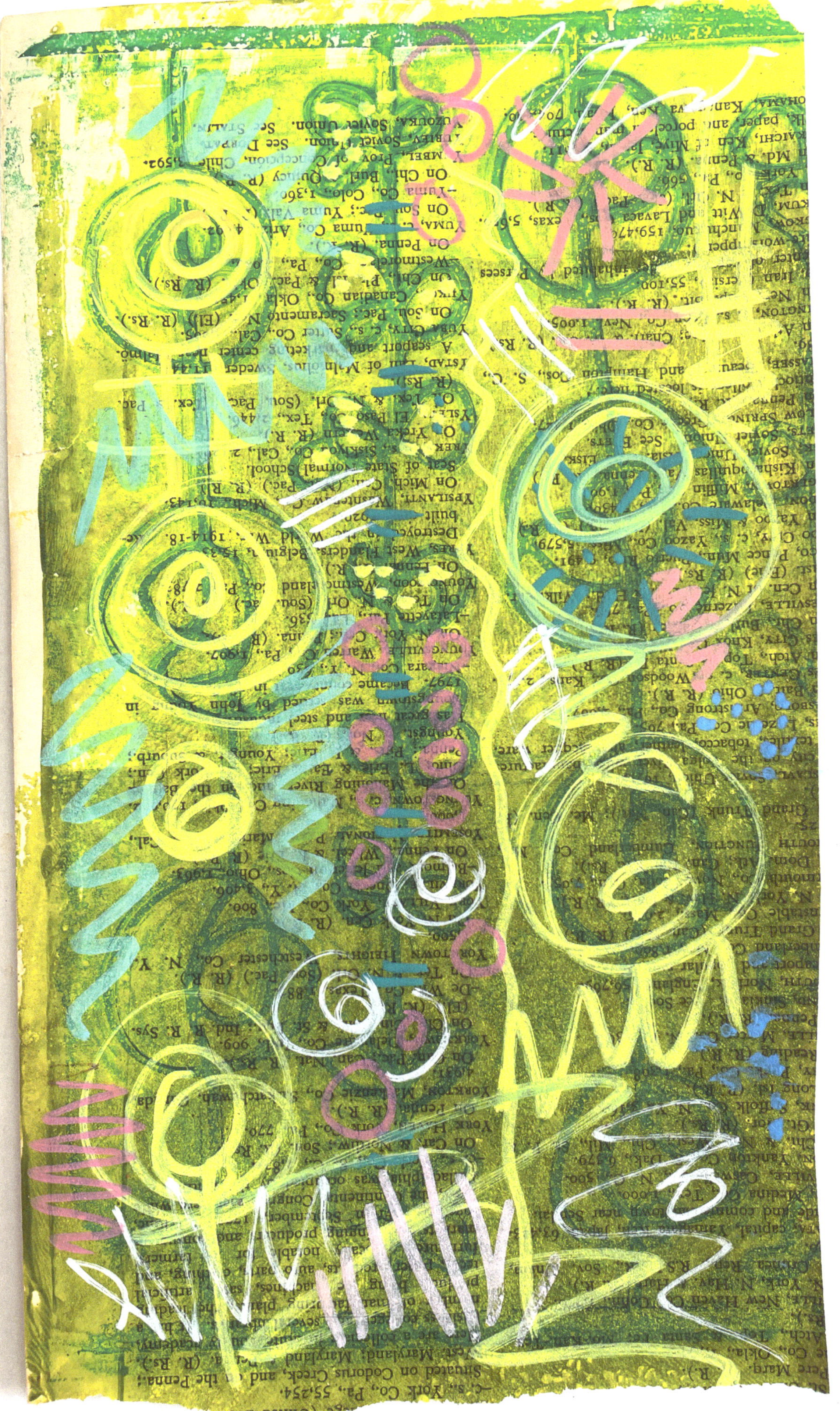

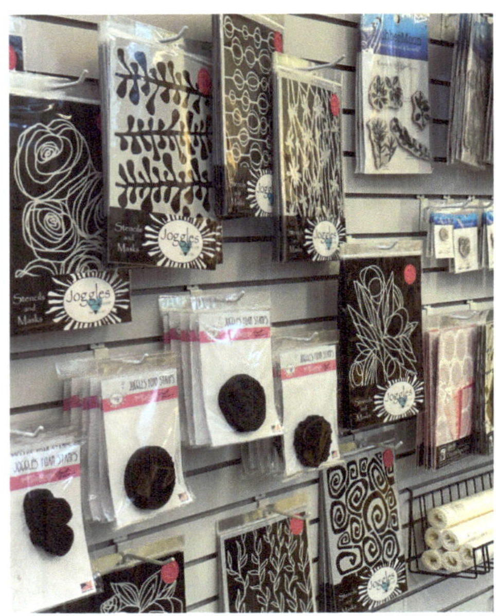

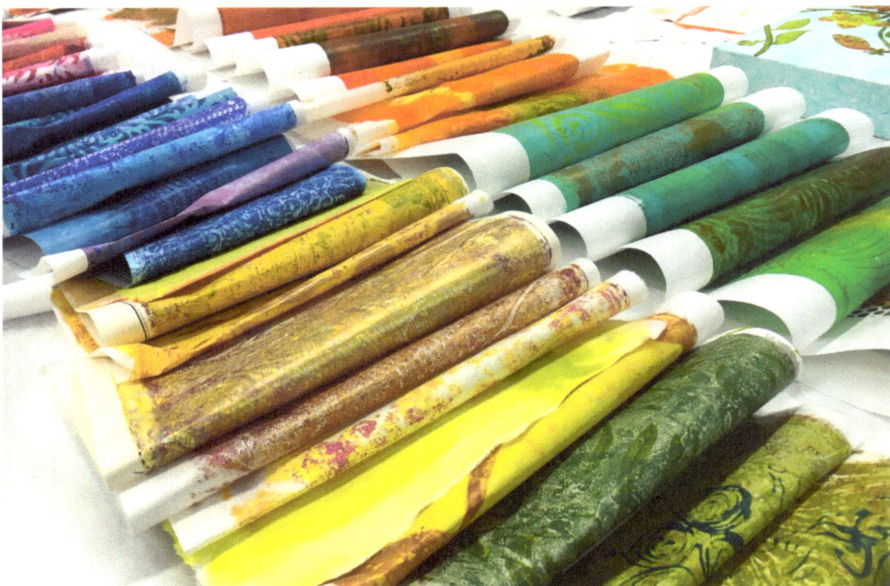

ABOUT THE AUTHOR

What sets the collage work of Elizabeth St. Hilaire apart is her use of unique, one-of-a-kind papers. Her signature collage style utilizes papers colored by hand, in every hue and texture needed to provide a complete paper palette.

View a full portfolio of the artists work at
PaperPaintings.com

Contact the artist via email at
Elizabeth@PaperPaintings.com

The Facebook studio page offers work in progress and workshop info
Facebook.com/PaperPaintingsCollageArtwork

Follow her Tutorial Tidbits via the blog at
PaperPaintings.com